HUG

CHAPTER ONE

COSTA DEL HUGO

"Whit's fucking happening here?!!"

"Whit's rang Hugo?"

"There's no fucking way I'm going back to Barlinnie, Davie."

Davie Little runs the drugs trade in Central and West Scotland. He's never done any jail time yet and for very good reason.

I'm just out the Bar-L and the cunt has just asked me to take a package to Spain for him. Me and Davie go way back. I've done courier runs to Liverpool for him but fuck me, Spain? What the fuck do I know about Spain?

There's nae way I'll get a job in this toon either. They all know my history, so I'm fucked. Who wants to hire a renowned drug courier? Nae cunt, that's who. It was Awright back in the 80's 'cause nae cunt cared. Now it's 1995 and it's a stigma if you hire somebody like me noo. It would burst ye man so it wid.

"Davie, I'm probably gonna regret this but give me all the details and I'm in. What the fuck else am I going to do man?"

"Good man Hugo, you'll no regret this wan. It'll be a good lift for you this, £10k."

Now ten thousand pounds would come in handy for me right now. It doesn't come in handy though when you're sat in a cell for eight fucking year. I need to be savvy here, use all my contacts and maybe this could work out for me.

"Right Hugo, I'll have a pre-loaded Ford Cortina that'll get you there no problem. The drugs will be in it sealed and sprayed so that the sniffer dogs at the Borders will never detect them. You'll leave in 48 hours, so square your shit away here that you need to do. Meet me here on Monday morning at 10am and I'll give you your schedule. I want you to take somebody with you, somebody you trust. It's a long fucking drive down there mate."

Right I've got two days to pick the right person here, I need to get to the pub and the bookies to narrow it down to a couple of the cunts then make my decision.

"Sadie!! A pint of your Scottish finest please, doll."

"A pint of me then son?"

"Fuck sake Sadie, a pint of Lager."

Sadie was about 70 odd, flirted with every cunt, but she never suffered fools gladly. She also wore the biggest pair of glasses known to man. Her husband, auld Bill, died about ten years ago so she started in here then. Wild horses couldn't get her out this pub. She'll leave here in a box bless her. This is her life now.

"Where's aw the boys the day Sadie?"

"They're aw et the Fitba the day Hugo mind? They said you had some meeting so that Jameson got your season ticket. They'll be in soon son."

"Fuck sake Sadie, so they are. I had other stuff on my mind."

"Aye, me, son probably," says a smirking Sadie.

The door to the pub bursts open and in walks the six boys. Tony, John, Colin, Donald, Pedro and Jameson. They see a concerned looking face on me instead of a happy one for a change.

"Whit's up wae your coupon?" says Colin

"Och I'll tell you later pal, I don't want to say too much in here the noo."

"Aw, right pal, I get what you mean. To do with your meeting today, aye?"

"Aye. Whit was the score Colin?"

"We won 1-0 Hugo, you never missed much."

"Jameson, c'mere tae a talk to you, over here."

"Whit's rang Hugo?"

Jameson looks visibly shaken cause he knows how volatile Hugo can be.

"Have you got my season ticket there?"

"Aye, Hugo it's here."

Jameson gets it out of his wallet and tries to pass it to Hugo.

"Keep it, it's yours Jameson. I need to go away in two days. You keep it until I get back, ok?"

"Errrrm, ok Hugo, no bother big man."

The mood in the pub isn't a good one. The boys all know that there's something up with Hugo but everybody is too scared to ask him. They continue to guzzle the beer and have banter with Sadie and Hugo slips off to the bookies.

Robert has been in the bookies for nearly twenty years. He's a miserable auld bastard and due to retire. He's been telling me all week about the new boy that's starting today, so I'd better pop in and introduce myself.

"Roberto!! Whit's the script auld yin? Is that yer boy?"

"His name is Thomas actually Hugo and no, he's not my boy. Thomas this is Hugo, one of our regulars."

"Awright wee man, yer name is Tam from noo on, pleased to meet ye."

I canny see this wee guy Tam lasting here. Not after getting a handover from that auld miserable bastard. The poor boy won't last the week.

"It's awfy quiet Roberto, naebody been in the day? Who's the auld fella in the corner wi the bunnet on?"

"Some Irish guy called James, a nice fella. He's emptied my fecking till today though. The new Parish Priest, Father Jackson was in too today to introduce himself. The boys were in earlier as well to put their bets on before they went to the football. Barring that, it's been quiet."

I'm not gonna get anybody in here to come with me and there's no way I'm taking that auld miserable cunto Roberto with me. I better get back over to the pub and make my decision.

When I walk back into the pub, everybody is fucking steaming. John, Colin and Tony are nearly having a punch-up, arguing about the fitba. Jameson is naewhere to be seen and Donald and Pedro who are both brothers, are having a family reminiscing moment in the corner greeting.

"I love you, naw, I love you."

I'm away doon the road. I'll make my decision tomorrow when everybody is sober. Sadie gives me a look with her big spunk deflectors on and blows me a kiss as I say cheerio. I've got a big decision to make tomorrow so it needs to be the right person. Spain here we come!!

CHAPTER TWO

THE DECISION

It's Sunday morning and I'm heading down the main street back down to the pub. The boys were all drinking last night so I know for a fact that they'll be down for a curer. I've narrowed it down to five. I don't really know or trust that Jameson, so it's between the five other boys. They'll all say aye, I've done enough favours for them over the years.

"Hugo!!" A wee voice shouts me from across the other side of the road.

"JJ!! You stay there with your mammy son, I'll cross over."

JJ is only four years old. His mother Terry is a lovely woman. I gave him a pound note one day last year walking through the toon. I canny walk past the wee shite now without giving him a pound, so every time he sees me he shouts me.

"How ye getting on Hugo?" says Terry

"Aye I'm no bad hen, I'm off to Spain the morra for a wee bit of sun."

"No' bad for some. We're just out of mass there. We got a new priest the other day. An Irish fella, named Father Jackson."

"Aye, Roberto from the bookies said yous had a new one up at the Pineapple."

"Chapel. Hugo, the Chapel."

"Haha, sorry Terry, I need to shoot off hen, I'm meeting the boys at the pub."

"Enjoy Spain Hugo!!"

That wee shite JJ is staunin' there with his paw oot, so that's me another pound note light.

"Sadie!! A pint of lager please doll."

"Hugo!!"

"Donald!! Pedro!! Might've known you two would be in here, Where's the other boys?"

"Didn't you hear?" said Pedro. Tony & John started fighting after you and Colin left the pub. Both of them are in the hospital. It's nothing major, just cuts and bruises. It was handbags at dawn, they were both steaming."

"Fuck sake."

I'm just in the pub and that rules they two daft bastards out straight away. Two guys with cuts and bruises all over their faces will stand out a mile at the border crossings.

"Donald!! Pedro!! Huuuuuuuuuugo!!"

Colin bounces in all pleased with himself.

"Whit's up with your chops, Coco?" says Donald.

"The good lady Sanny is still asleep. She told me under no circumstances have I to go to the pub today. So, being the gentleman that I am, I've fucking snuck out the hoose. I'll show her who's the boss in that house lads!!"

"Wheeeey!!!" is the noise from all the men in the pub.

"Right lads I need to talk to yous before yous get wellied in to the beer. I need to drive to Spain the morra; drop a car off and then we'll fly back. I need one of you three to come with me. I'll give you a thousand pounds to do it as well, plus I'll pay for everything."

"Fuck Hugo. I'd love to mate, but I've no' got a Passport," says Pedro

"Right, it needs to one of you two then. I need an answer in the next hour before yous get pished. Once I get the answer, get up the road and pack your shit."

"A thousand pound to drop a motor off Hugo, what is it? A Ferrari?," says Donald.

"Naw. It's a Ford Cortina, Donald."

"Right, whit's in it Hugo? It better no be fucking drugs, man?"

"Don't you fucking concern yourself with what's in it. Wan of you two are dain' it and that's fucking it, ok?"

They both put their heids doon, cause they know I'm serious. One of these two are coming with me and that's it. Just as I'm about to go on another rant, the pub phone goes. It's the loudest fucking phone in NATO, cause it's usually busy in here.

"Colin!! Is there a Colin in here?" shouts Sadie

Colin's looking at her and shakes his heid as if to say, hell fucking no, there's definitely no Colin in here.

"Naw hen, there's no Colin in here, sorry," says Sadie to the person on the other end of the phone.

I shoot to the bar to buy the boys a round of drinks. As I'm standing at the bar, Colin and Donald are looking worried. Pedro's no' giving two fucks because he's not got a passport. I'm just about to pick the pints up off the bar to take them to the table, when suddenly the front doors burst open.

"Hawl, Prick!!"

There's this woman stood at the front door not looking very happy and she's looking straight in Colin's direction.

"Sanny!!" says Colin sheepishly

"You've got two seconds to get your arse oot this bar and up the road, afore a punch yer cunt in right in front of everybody."

"Coming Sanny!!"

"Wheeeey!!!" screams all the guys in the pub.

,"Aye ye certainly fucking showed her who's boss," screams wee Alberto from the end of the bar.

I give wee Alberto Colin's pint for his patter, but as I get back to the table, Donald knows that he's fucked.

"Tough fucking tittie Donald, it looks like it's you pal. Once you've finished this pint, get up the road, pack your shit and meet me at Longshanks yard at 10am tomorrow morning, good to go, ok?"

"Ok Hugo."

That's that then, Donald is coming with me to Spain. We meet at Longshanks yard tomorrow morning at 10am,, to pick up the Cortina packed with drugs. £9k to me and £1k to him. Straight to Spain drop the car off then fly straight back. The easiest money we'll both make. Nothing could possibly wrong now, could it?

CHAPTER THREE

DONALD WHERE'S YER TROOSERS

"Toothbrush, wallet, passport and suitcase. Sorted Hugo son, sorted."

Now I hate going abroad. The last time I was abroad was for Italia 90, five years ago, to watch Scotland get pumped by Costa Rica, beat Sweden and then get beat by Brazil. Juan Cayasso scoring that winner for Costa Rica will haunt me for the rest of my life.

Out of the five guys I could've picked, Donald would probably have been the last because he bores the tits right aff ye man - but, needs must. I can trust the cunt. I better get doon to Longshanks yard, it's hawf nine.

I turn up at the yard and there's two motors already parked up outside the gates. A brand new Mercedes and a fine looking Ford Cortina. This bodybuilder opens the back door of the Merc as I'm walking towards the gate and out steps Davie Little. AKA, The Iceman. He was nicknamed that not because he was just cool as fuck, his eyes send a shiver down yer spine.

"Hugo!! Are you all set mate?"

"Aye, Davie, I'm good to go man. I just need the itenary and maps etc. and I'm all set."

"Who's going with you Hugo? It's a long journey down there and I can't afford you falling asleep at the wheel with Two Million Pounds worth of merchandise in the car now can I?"

"My pal Donald, should be here any minute Davie."

"Ok, here's your itenary, phone numbers and maps. Follow it all to the book and everything will work out just fine. You'll be back here in a week, with £10k to play with Hugo. Here's some Francs and some Peseta's for hotels and petrol for you both too. I'll give you the usual, half now and half when the job is done. Here's your first £5k in this envelope.

"If you take your time, you can do it in four days. Or if you want to get there and back, do it in shifts and you could be done in two. I'll leave it up to you, but I'll give you one warning Hugo, don't fuck this up."

"Fuck sake Davie, you know I won't."

"Who's this clown walking towards us in shorts, Hugo?"

"Fuck sake, it's Donald."

"**Donald where's yer troosers**!!" sings Davie

"I thought we were going to Spain?" says Donald

"Aye we're no' fucking well there yet, ya buffoon ye!!" shouts Hugo

"Now, now boys, don't argue before the journey has even started. Good luck and God speed lads. Phone me when the job is done Hugo. Cheerio. Oh, one last thing Hugo. My wee nephew Kris Little works doon there in a bank, if you bump into him, look after him eh?"

"Aye, nae bother Davie."

When the fuck am I gonna have time to bump into his nephew fur fuck sake? Straight there and straight back. The big cunt slams the back door of the Merc and it then speeds away. Me and Donald are stood outside Longshanks yard and this fucking eejit has got a pair of shorts on and it's Baltic. You couldn't write this. This is going to be one long fucking journey, man.

We put the bags in the boot of the Cortina. I give Donald the UK Map for the first leg of our journey down to Dover. We decide we're just going to do the full stretch in turns. I check the itinerary. It reads as follows.

HUGO

WHEN YOU ARRIVE IN SPAIN, CONTACT THE FOLLOWING PERSON.

GUSTAVO RAMIREZ. HIS NUMBER IS 0034 635 91 70 15

I'VE HIGHLIGHTED THE CITY ON THE SPANISH MAP THAT YOU NEED TO HEAD TO. IT'S CALLED La Linea. THE MEETING PLACE FOR YOU TO DELIVER THE CAR IS THE MAIN HOSPITAL. IT'S SIGN POSTED EVERYWHERE NO MATTER WHICH WAY YOU COME IN FROM. AGAIN, CONTACT GUSTAVO AS YOU ARRIVE AND HE WILL MEET YOU THERE.

ONCE YOU HAVE HANDED OVER THE CAR TO GUSTAVO, CONTACT MYSELF ON MY HOUSE PHONE AND MAKE YOUR WAY BACK TO SCOTLAND FOR PAYMENT FOR THE CAR.

IF YOU NEED ANYTHING WHILST IN SPAIN, GUSTAVO WILL HELP YOU OUT.

THE ICEMAN

"Right, Donald get that fucking Spanish map oot to Ah see where this City is."

Donald opens each envelope until he finds the Spanish Map.

Hugo opens it right up and starts scouring it from the top and works his way down looking for the highlighted marker.

"Whit's goin' on here, fur fuck sake?!!"

"Whit's the matter, Hugo?"

"It's right doon the fucking bottom of Spain man. It's right ootside Gibraltar, fur fuck sake. We're nearly driving to Africa here, man!!"

"Och, it'll be an adventure Hugo!!"

"I'm gonnae fucking strangle you Donald and we haven't even set aff yet. Right, let's get the show on the road. Get that map in your face and don't fucking bug the life oot of me Donald."

"Ok Hugo."

The boys head off towards the M8 and then head down towards Carlisle. It's not long before Donald starts bugging Hugo.

"Is there bookies in Spain, Hugo?"

"How the fuck would a know Donald, I've never been."

"It's just my brother gave me a few tips for the racing on Saturday."

"We'll be back in Scotland on fucking Saturday so don't worry about it. You can bug the life out the new boy,, Tam in the bookies then."

Donald decides it's best to keep his mouth shut until they reach Liverpool when Hugo informs him that it's his turn to drive. They stop at a service station where Hugo used to do his drug drops. They have a wee bite to eat, a coffee and hit the road again.

"Eh, Hugo."

"Whit, Donald?"

"Can you get the map oot so I know where we're going please?"

"It's a straight road now all the way down. We cannae get fucking loast, we're on an island. Just keep heading South and pick up the signs for Dover. I'm going for a kip."

The boys arrive in Dover just before 9pm. A near 500 mile journey and with the stop, they done it in good time. Donald gives Hugo a slight nudge.

"Hugo!!"

"Oh ya cunt, whit?"

"We're here man, wake up. I'm shiteing maself here. I don't know if I can dae this, Hugo."

"Stop being a fanny Donald, it'll be plain sailing. I'll get the tickets for the boat then I'll drive us through customs."

Hugo disappears into the Ticket Office, Donald is shaking like a shitting dog. The next couple of hours will determine if they're Scot free into France or in a jail cell for the next ten years plus.

CHAPTER FOUR

BANGED UP ABROAD

Hugo emerges from the ticket office and Donald is nowhere to be seen in the car park.

"See if that cun'ts done a runner, I'll fucking kill him."

Ten minutes later, Donald appears looking as white as a ghost.

"Where the fuck have you been, Casper?"

"Hugo, I've been for two shites and spewed my ring up four times. I know this is second nature to you, but the worst thing I've ever done is stolen my next door neighbours' knickers and sniffed them with Pedro."

"Gads a fuck you man. Gie it a by eh? We'll be absolutely, fine ya trumpet. Get in the fucking motor afore we miss this Ferry.

"Right, Donald, drink some of that water in the back seat, relax and kid on yer sleeping. I'll dae all the talking at customs. Give me your passport tae and I'll sort everything."

"I'm just shiteing it mate, don't tell the boys back hame eh? I don't want to be banged up abroad with some French guy called Pierre flinging his ten inch dong up ma farter."

"Go tae sleep ya dick."

The boys go through passport control, Hugo flashes the two passports and he gets the hand signal to progress. They then head towards customs. Polis are everywhere with all their dugs sniffing each car as it comes through. The boys are next up. Hugo drives up and the two German Shepherds get to work on the Cortina.

"Clear!!," shouts one of the coppers and the boys queue up for the Ferry in their row.

"See Casper, everything is fine pal. We've got one more Customs team to get through in France and then we're Scot free. I've got a clove of garlic in my bag for they cunts, once they smell that, we'll be straight through."

The boys settle down on the ferry for the crossing. They get another bite to eat, Donald has another two shites and they're all set for their last hurdle. French Customs!! They get back into the Cortina. Hugo takes the wheel again so that Casper doesn't get them rumbled.

"Right, last bit here. We got through the strictest customs oot there. These French cunts will be dying for their next baguette Donald. Same deal as last time ok? Get yer Aberdeen Angus heid doon."

Hugo approaches the Passport control. He passes the two passports over. The guy scans Donald's first, nods and hands it back. He then scans Hugo's, scan's it again and then again a third time.

"Turn your engine off and both of you, step outside the car please! "Now!!"

The Polis surround our motor, the two of us are flung up against a wall and a policeman drives the car into a parking bay. We're fucked, totally fucked!! We get separated, Donald goes with two coppers and doesn't get put into handcuffs. I do get put into handcuffs and taken away as well by two French cops.

I'm led into an interview room and can see Donald through the clear glass. I'm in an interview room and he's sitting in the waiting room. I'm in cuffs and he's no'.

"Whit's goin' fucking oan here?!!"

Hunners of things are going through my heid here. Did that cunt grass me in at the other side to get himself aff with this. My mind is in fucking overdrive for half an hour when, suddenly, two French guys in suits appear in the interview room clutching paperwork.

"There's an International arrest warrant out for you Hugo, outstanding from 1990."

"Eh?"

"Did you, or did you no,t assault a Mr Juan Cayasso in the Luigi Ferraris Stadium in Genoa, Italy, with a Ham & Cheese sandwich, on the evening of the 11th of June, 1990?"

Hugo bursts out laughing.

"Aye, Ah did, the cunt scored against Scotland for Costa Rica - so Ah flung a piece at him and scudded him right on the back of the nut with it. The Polis seen me and lifted me, this has all been dealt wi'   ."

"We hardly got any of that, in English please?"

Hugo starts to explain the night in question over and over again and after a few phone calls in the morning to his lawyer, the matter was cleared up and the boys were free to go.

"I got closer to that cunt than any of the Scottish defenders that night, Donald. Let's go pal."

The boys go on their merry way. Donald starts to relax as they hit the open road. The boys are shattered, so they decide to get an hotel with underground parking to get some shut eye for a few hours, before they hit the road again.

"Right, up you get Donald. This is going to be a cunt of a drive this wan. We'll drive all the way to Madrid from here and we'll do it over two legs, again. That hold up at Customs has set us back about eight hours. Let's get to Madrid and phone Gustavo. We'll get a good kip there and then get on our final leg to LA, whatever it's called."

"Sounds good to me Hugo."

The lads batter on, to Madrid and again, find a nice hotel with underground parking for the car stuffed with drugs. It's just over 300 miles from Madrid to La Linea, so they're on the final stretch now.

"Right Donald, get your heid down mate. I'll phone this Gustavo and let him know we're here. No' long now, bud, and we'll be heading back to Scotland, pal."

"Aye, thank fuck, Hugo."

Hugo uses the phone in his bedroom and dials the number that Davie gave him. It rings about five times then this Spanish guy picks up the phone.

"Hola!!"

"Aye, hello!! It's Hugo here.Ccan I speak to Gustavo, please?"

"Que pasa, Hugo, it's Gustavo here, how are you my friend?"

"Aye, magic Gustavo. Righ,t Amigo, we're in Madrid. We're gonna get some sleep then we'll head down to La Linea ma man. We should be there in around twelve hours time, ok?"

"Si, si that's perfecto Hugo, my friend. Call me when you reach La Linea."

"Aye nae bother, Gustavo. See you later pal."

"Adios, Hugo."

The phone goes dead and Hugo climbs into bed. It's been an eventful couple of days for the boys. They're shattered and they need their rest. This is the last part of their journey and when they wake up, they can do this last 300 mile drive and then it's Scotland bound again.

CHAPTER FIVE

VILLAGE OF THE DAMNED

"Donald we've fucking slept in man, get up! "It's nearly 8pm, we'll no' get there until through the night noo. I'll phone Gustavo. You get the hotel sorted out and get the motor started up. I telt ye to get me up at four ya thundercunt."

Hugo goes next door to his room to phone Gustavo and Donald rushes about like a madman to pay the bill and start the car up. Next stop, La Linea.

The boys drive for just over five hours and finally reach the La Linea sign. As they drive in, there's a petrol station so Hugo pops in to see if they have a phone to call Gustavo. Thankfully they do and Hugo uses the last of the Pesetas that Davie gave them to give Gustavo a call.

"Hola."

"Gustavo, it's Hugo mate, we're here."

"Where? La Linea?"

"Yes, pal."

"Ok, I'm in bed, but give me 15 minutes and I'll meet you at the hospital."

"Ok no problem, we seen a sign for it as we drove in. See you soon Gustavo."

"Si, Adios Hugo."

This is it, we're 15 minutes away from handing this motor over and the getting the fuck out of Dodge. I didn't think I'd miss auld Sadie and her gargantuan spunk deflectors as much as I do, but get me fucking hame, pronto.

We pull up outside the Hospital and it's fucking creepy. I mean really fucking creepy. I'm no' kidding ye on. T|here's genuine, real life zombies walking past our motor, fucked oot their heid. Hurry up, Gustavo, this place is giving me the fear here. It's like the village of the damned.

Finally some headlights in the rear view mirror and this car pulls in behind us. Two guys get out. Please God be Gustavo!!

"Hugo, I'm Gustavo. This is my partner, Pepe."

"Gustavo, thank fuck man. I thought I was in a Zombie film there."

"Ah, I see you've met some of the locals already?"

"Yes, we have indeed."

"Ok, I need you to empty everything of yours out of the car. Gibraltar is approximately three miles in that direction. You'll either get a taxi to Malaga airport from the border, or you'll get a nice hotel in Gibraltar for the night."

"Wait a minute here Gustavo. We've got our suitcases and approximately five grand in cash on us. Will we even make it the three miles? Can't you at least give us a lift?"

"We can't, we must go straight away with the merchandise. Our boss is waiting for it now. We must go. I'm sorry, Hugo."

"Taxi, get us a taxi then Gustavo. Something here, fur fuck sake."

"Hugo, taxi's don't come to this part of town. Bye."

Gustavo speeds away in his car and Pepe drives the Cortina. The two of us are left outside La Linea hospital, at nearly 2am and the place is hoaching with drug addicts. This three mile gauntlet of zombies is just what the doctor ordered after that journey.

"Right you, stop shiteing yersell again, Donald. It is what it is, let's boost on man."

"Hugo, I've got a bad feeling about this."

"Move yer arse, Donald!!"

The boys don't even get 20 metres and somebody stops them asking them for money. If it's not for money it's for sex and if it's not for sex, it's for fags. This continues for nearly two miles and the Spaniards must be fluent in "get to fuck" by now, because that's all Hugo has been saying for the past half an hour.

They can see the red flashing lights on the Rock of Gibraltar now, so they know that they're getting close. They only have one more estate to walk through now and they're home clear. Suddenly around twenty people surround us in this estate. Shouting at us in Spanish and neither of the two of us have a clue what they're saying. Then, suddenly, I belt out those famous Scottish words.

"Mon then, ya cunts!!"

I charge into a section of the crowd, I get about four of them down in seconds, but then the crowd race me and I'm done for. A couple of them deal with Donald. But, like a pack of Hyena's it's over in the matter of seconds.

"Hugo, Hugo, Hugo. Waken up, will ye?"

Poor Donald is shaking Hugo, trying to wake him up and wiping the blood off his face with his t-shirt. Hugo starts to stir.

"Oh thank fuck Hugo. I thought ye were deid. You're fucking crazy man so ye ur!!"

Hugo springs up.

"Where are the cunts, eh?"

"Sit doon for a minute eh, ye took a bit of a doing there mucker."

Donald starts to explain what happened.

"They've took everything Hugo. Our luggage, our passports and our money."

"The wee bastards. Wait till I get my hauns on them all."

"What are we going to do Hugo? We're in the middle of an estate in the arse end of Spain with absolutely fuck all."

Donald starts greeting.

"Right haud the bus man, check yer pockets, Donald."

"I already huv Hugo, they've took everything."

Hugo checks his and yes, they have taken everything. Except one thing, the itinerary.

"Gustavo!! Ya fucking beauty!! Right Donald, on yer feet son. Let's get to the safety of that Gibraltar border; explain the situation to the Polis and use a phone to contact Gustavo and Davie and let them know what's happening. We'll be on a flight oot of here tomorrow, you mark my words, Donald."

"Withoot a passport Hugo?"

"Oh aye, shit!!"

CHAPTER SIX

THE QUEEN OF La Linea

We get the Spanish National Polis at the Gibraltar border to speak with the UK Polis and we explain our situation. We manage to get through the border and they summon an ambulance for me. I didn't want to get in it, but they insisted due to my blood loss. I get cleaned up at the hospital and after some X-Rays, I get the all clear.

The Sister in charge asks me if I need to phone anybody and I tell her that I do. Gustavo was a bit of a prick the last time I met him so he better not fucking piss me off again. We need money and a passport. I'll also need to phone Davie back home and explain everything.

"Hola."

"Gustavo it's Hugo."

"Hugo, what can I do for you?"

"Quite a fucking lot at this moment in time actually. We got fucking battered just before the Gibraltar border in some estate, by about twenty folk. They've stolen everything. Our money, our luggage and more importantly, our passports. We're at the hospital in Gibraltar with absolutely nothing and we need your help, Gustavo."

"Oh my God, Hugo, are you both ok?"

"Donald is fine. I took a bit of a doing, but I'll be ok. Can you come for us?"

"I can't as I'm still dealing with this merchandise, but I'll send Pepe right away Wait outside the hospital and Pepe will be there, in approximately an hour, with the border queue."

"Perfect,, Gustavo cheers."

"No problem Hugo, I'll catch up with you later, Amigo."

"What did he say, Hugo?" asks Donald.

"He'll be here for us in an hour, Donald. I'll need to phone Davie now and let him know what's happened. This will be fun.

Hullo. Davie, it's Hugo man and I've got some good news and some bad news for you."

"I don't like bad news Hugo, you know that."

"Don't worry Davie, we dropped off the merchandise. Gustavo left us to get to Gibraltar from the rendezvous point and we got our cunts kicked in by some locals just before the Gibraltar border.

"They took our luggage, our money and our passports fur fuck sake. I've literally just checked out of the hospital there. We're baith fine, but been left with nothing here, Davie."

"Right Hugo, don't worry about it. I'm sorry to hear about your predicament. I'll contact Gustavo's boss and get her to sort you out with everything Is that prick Gustavo coming for you?"

"Oh, I'm glad you think he's a prick tae. He left us in the fucking middle of the village of the damned to get our cunts kicked in."

"Ah La Linea, happy memories Hugo. It was a lovely wee place until Gustavo got his hands on it."

"Whit? Do you mean his boss is a burd anaw Davie?"

"Aye, Miss G!! The Queen of La Linea. Nobody has ever met her but she controls everything there."

"Interesting stuff Davie. Thanks for that wee bit of info and I'll be keeping that Gustavo cunt at arms length until this passport situation is sorted out.ccI'll hopefully see you soon."

"Don't worry about a thing down there now, Miss G owes me some favours."

"Cheers, boss."

Hugo explains everything to Donald and they both perk up a bit. The nurses sort them out with a coffee, some water and a bit of food. They then make there way outside as Pepe should be here any minute now.

"Where do you think they'll take us Hugo?"

"Fuck knows Donald but Davie said that we've not to worry so that'll do me. This Miss G character is going to look after us apparently so we'll see. One last thing Donald, keep an eye on that Gustavo cunt, he's for the watching."

"Ok Hugo."

Just at that, a big BMW with Spanish plates comes screeching round the corner. It's Pepe.

"Amigos, get in."

"Pepe, this is Donald, Donald, Pepe," says Hugo. Where are you taking us Pepe?"

"I've been instructed by my boss to take you to one of our safe houses up the coast. It's in the middle of nowhere, so you can chill for a couple of days, whilst Miss G sorts everything out for you."

"A couple of days Pepe? We want to go hame, son" says Donald.

"Hugo has been injured, they won't let him on a flight with his injuries anyway, Donald. It's best that you relax for a couple of days, until the swelling goes down. Like, I said, don't worry about a thing. Miss G will cater for all your needs here."

"Aye, right son" says Donald.

CHAPTER SEVEN

I LOVE MOROCCO HUGO

We leave the magnificent site of Gibraltar, drive back through La Linea and up the coast towards Malaga. We arrive in a place called "*Sotogrande*" and Pepe pulls up to these massive gates. There's two guys in suits, with walkie talkies, they open the gates and let us drive in. As we approach this huge villa with our mouths wide open, Pepe tells us that this is where we'll be lying low for a few days.

We pull up to the front door and there's these two amazing looking women standing there. Pepe opens the back door for us and we get out.

> "Hugo, Donald, this is Siham and Helima. They've both recently arrived from Morocco and they'll look after your every need whilst your here. Miss G has instructed them to do whatever you wish during your stay and they will The girls will show you around and take you to your rooms."

Siham takes Hugo hand and Helima takes Donald's. The ladies give the boys a grand tour of the villa and then show them to their respective rooms. The ladies tell the lads that food will be ready in twenty minutes. The boys get a shower, put their new robes on and head downstairs.

> "Fuck me Hugo, this is unreal this hoose. Wait till the boys hear about this."

> "Just shut it, Donald. My ribs are killing me here, fuck this hoose and fuck everything. I just want to get hame, man."

> "Hugo, Donald, help yourself," says Siham.

Now I've seen some spreads in my time, but these two lassies have honestly got enough food here to feed about ten folk. We blether away to our two new pals and start to get to know them better. Two lovely lassies not only to look at, but to talk to as well.

> "I give you massage now, Hugo," says Siham.

> "I'm a wee bit sore hen, but I wouldn't say no."

Siham proceeds to take Hugo up to his room to massage him and Helima follows suit with Donald. It's been a hectic few days for the lads. This wee bit of TLC is just what the doctor ordered.

The next morning Hugo wakes up beside Siham and he can't believe his luck. He just lies there and stares at her. Perfection, utter perfection he thinks to himself. He hobbles into the shower, still sore from his beating and Siham joins him. Hugo just can't believe his luck. As they finish off in the shower, the phone in his room starts ringing. Hugo hobbles through and picks it up.

"Hello."

"Hello, Hugo, this is Miss G. I assume you've heard of me?"

"Eh aye, I've heard your name mentioned."

"Ok, that should save me some time then. I hope you like your new surroundings and the girls are looking after you?"

"Aye magic Miss G, magic."

"Good. Hugo, I have a bit of a problem down here and Davie told me that you'd be the person to sort it out for me."

"Eh, whit problem is that?"

"Gustavo has turned what was once a lovely coast, into a desperate one. I want you to get rid of him for me and work for me Hugo."

"Whit? I'm supposed to be going back to Scotland, hopefully tomorrow."

"That won't be happening I'm afraid. I can offer you money that you could only have dreamt of. Girls, money, power, cars - the lot Hugo. Behind the drinks cabinet in your room, there's also a suitcase full of money. That's yours to do with as you please as well."

"Keep talking."

"I've set up a drugs meet for you to attend with Gustavo and Pepe in *Estepona*. They'll pick you up and drive you there tomorrow night. Nobody else will be there. If you look inside your bedside cabinet, I've put a pistol in there for you to use, with ten rounds already in the clip. Kill Gustavo, Hugo, and get back to the villa. Once it's done, get Siham to call me to let me know it's done.

I'll inform Pepe of the plan and he'll be your new right hand man Hugo. He'll show you everything here that'll get you started. I want you to take over Southern Spain and the Straits of Gibraltar. Turn this coast back to what it should be, Hugo. Pepe will get rid of his body for you, just shoot him Hugo."

"Fucking hell Miss G, I was just to drop off a Cortina here."

"There was nothing in the Cortina Hugo, it was my test for you to see if I could trust you. You passed the test."

"Ok, I'll do it Miss G. I canny stand that cunt Gustavo anyway, so I might actually enjoy this. I've got nothing to go hame for anyway, so this might actually work out down here."

"Ok Hugo, I'll look forward to Siham's call tomorrow night."

"Ok Miss G, thanks for this opportunity here, I won't let you down."

"Bye Hugo."

I'm no' long oot Bar-L, with no job and no prospects and now I'm being offered to control the whole of Southern Spain. I've got a stunning 21 year old Moroccan lassie on tap and I'm staying in a luxury villa. Somebody fucking pinch me here. I haven't heard or seen Donald this morning, I better go and see what he's up to.

"Donald! Donald! Where are you, ya mad cunt?"

"Hugo, I'm in the Jacuzzi, ootside man"!

I lean over my balcony and there's Donald in the jacuzzi with Helima straddling him. She's riding him like a grand national winner.

"I love Morocco, Hugo!!"

"Fuck sake, Donald."

"What's going on out there, Hugo?" ask Siham

"Oh, nothing."

I better get myself prepared for the morra night. I'll enjoy today with Siham and the Jacuzzi Two. Then it's time to get the serious heid on. I don't like that cunt Gustavo for just leaving us in the village of the damned. If I can change this coast for the better, then I will. First step, no more Gustavo.

CHAPTER EIGHT

YER NO' A BAD CUNT DONALD

I need to let Donald know about the situation. The poor cunt, like me, thought he was going home tomorrow. I take him away from the girls and explain the situation to him.

"Och, no way, Hugo!!"

"I'm afraid so mate. Look, once the money starts coming in, there's no reason why you can't go hame when you want."

"Aye, I suppose so, Hugo."

"Enjoy this place; enjoy Helima and I'll give you a nice wedge to go home with mate,ok?"

"Spot on Hugo, cheers."

Once Donald digests the news, we send the lassies out to get us booze. We're going to party with the girls tonight and enjoy ourselves before our lives change tomorrow.

The Moroccon girls get back and bring us a mountain of booze. We get the music going and start to get wellied into the booze. We all get in the pool and have a laugh. Dunking the girls and dive bombing away. As we're in the pool, the housekeeper comes out.

"Hugo! Hugo! The telephone for you."

The music is fucking blaring downstairs so I head up to my room. I pick up the phone and it's Pepe.

"Hugo, Miss G has explained the situation to me After what Gustavo did by setting up those people up to attack you in *La Linea*, I'll be happy to help you tomorrow night."

"Whit, the dirty bastard?"

"Yes, they owed him money for drugs, so he made them all attack you. They dropped him off the £5000 from you as well and that paid their debt."

"I fecking knew he was up to something. I'm going to enjoy this."

"Ok Hugo, I pick you up at 9pm tomorrow so that it's just getting dark. I know the spot well, where we'll kill him. I have plastic sheeting in the boot already. I see you tomorrow nigh,t my friend."

"Yes, Pepe, looking forward to it now."

I'm fucking raging with Gustavo. Pulling this trigger tomorrow night will be easy now. He took a liberty with me there and I'm not having that. I head back out to the pool.

"Donald!"

"Aye, Hugo."

"Do you know that attack the other night in La Linea was set up by Gustavo?"

"Whit?"

"Aye, the folk in that estate owed him money, so he got them to attack us and hand him the money that Davie gave us."

"The dirty bastard, man."

"Aye, well don't worry, we'll get it back, and more, tomorrow night."

"Hugo, do you want me to come with you tomorrow night pal. I got a doing too because of that prick."

"Naw, Donald, you stay here with the girls mate. I won't be long with him don't worry. Yer no a bad cunt, Donald. Cheers for having my back."

"No problem Hug. How many times have you had mine?"

"Aye."

Siham motions me to go over to her at the other end of the pool. As I get closer, I honestly can't believe how gorgeous she is. Her jet black hair is soaking wet and her perfect body is glistening in the roasting hot Spanish sun.

"Hugo, get in here with me," she says.

I get into the pool and she wraps her arms and legs round me.

"Hugo, how long are you here for?"

"A while, Siham, a while."

"I want to stay here with you, I don't want to go back to Morocco next week."

"Next week?"

"Yes, Miss G asked Helima and I to come over here for one week and paid us excellent money. We've never worked for her before, but our boss Mustapha, who controls the drugs trade in Morocco, controls that side for her. He offered us a years wages to come here.

"It's not about the money anymore for me Hugo. I really like you and I'm falling for you. Can you speak with Miss G or Mustapha and see if I can stay? Please?"

"I'll see what I can do Siham, I'm falling for you too, you're amazing."

I've never really had a girl before. Plenty of one night stands and a month here and a month there, type of thing. Siham is something out of a film. Perfect in every single way and she's falling for a dafty like me? I'd be stupid to let her go back to Morocco.

"Hugo"!

"Whit Donald?"

"Me and Helima are going in the jacuzzi." Yous two coming?"

"Are we fuck going anywhere near that jacuzzi, ya dirty bastards."

CHAPTER NINE

GUSTAVO NO MORE

We all wake up to the noise of the huge wooden front door slamming shut. That'll be the housekeeper in. Siham turns round, and yet again, I can't quite believe my luck. Her perfect face just stares at me. I need to get out of lovey-dovey mode soon. Things are about to get more sinister.

We all toddle downstairs and the girls get the breakfast on. Donald looks like a kid in a sweetie shop with Helima too. Maybe this isn't such a bad idea being down here after all. I'm starting to really like Donald too, he's not as much of a boring bastard as I thought he was.

"Whit's the script today then, Hugo?"

"Once we've had breakfast Donald, we'll just chill out with the girls again this afternoon. Pepe is coming for me at 9pm. I want you to take the girls out for dinner at 8pm and get back here for 11pm ok?"

"Sure Hugo, no bother pal."

"There's a suitcase behind my drinks cabinet - with money in it. Take whatever you need and get the girls some nice food. Siham needs to phone Miss G though when I get back, so be back here no later than 11pm, ok?"

"We'll be here man, don't worry."

"Good."

We have another lovely breakfast with the girls. Donald looks more in love with Helima than I do with Siham. We spend another couple of hours in the pool and then retire to our rooms. Siham starts getting ready in front of me for her meal and I can't take my eyes off her. I'm one lucky man, hopefully she can stay.

"Right Siham, our taxi is here. Are you ready doll?" Donald shouts from outside the room.

"Coming Donald."

Siham gives me a kiss and wishes me good luck. This is it, game face time. This cunt is getting it.

I check the gun is loaded properly and take the safety catch off. I'm not wasting any time. As soon as we get there, the cunt is getting the full ten rounds in him. I hear a beep of the horn and look over the balcony. It's them, they're here.

,"Hugo my friend!" says Gustavo, as I walk down the steps to the car.

"Gustavo, how are you?"

I just want to leather the cunt right now.

"Miss G tells me that you are going to be sticking around for a while now and I've to show you the ropes here?"

"She told you that?"

"Yes my friend. I've to take you on this deal tonight and introduce you to our Russian friends up the coast."

"Ah, ok, yes, she did mention something about a deal. Looking forward to it Gustavo."

I get in the back seat of the car and Pepe is driving. He gives me a wee nod in the rear view mirror as if to say, we know what's going on here but Gustavo, you're fucked pal. We set off for Estepona.

Gustavo turns his attentions to the girls in the villa.

"So Hugo, how are you enjoying those two Moroccan sluts?"

"Ermmm... I wouldn't call them sluts, Gustavo. They're two really nice girls actually."

"Nice girls hahahahaha? I could load them onto a rib in La Linea tomorrow and throw them overboard on the way to Morocco and they'd never be seen again! "Nice girls... haha."

My blood is boiling now! This cunt not only got me a kicking and stole my money, but he's basically threatening those two lovely Moroccan lassies. Get me to Estepona now!

We hit the Estepona sign and turn off up this back-street and up a big hill. We park up in this quiet and secluded area.

"The Russians should be here any minute," says Gustavo.

"The Russians won't be here ya prick! Not only did you get me a kicking; steal five grand from me and my friend; but you go on to threaten two helpless wee lassies. You're fucking vermin man, and I'm the man to exterminate you."

I fire two shots into his stomach and he hits the floor. I then walk up to him.

"I've been told all about you Gustavo. You're the cancer that's killing people on this coast and ruining people's lives. I'm going to change that. Catch ye, ya fanny."

I empty the remaining eight rounds into him and to be honest, I've never felt better. This guy was scum of the highest order. I help Pepe lift the fat cunt into the boot of the motor and Pepe drives me home. We're both laughing and joking on the way back to the villa. Pepe says that he'll come and see me tomorrow.

It's 10.45pm now so I jump in a quick shower. I've got that fat cunts blood all over me and don't want Siham to see it when she gets in. I throw my clothes and trainers into the fire in the living room and I can see the Taxi coming up the driveway. I quickly clean the pistol and put it back in the bedside cabinet and run down to the front door.

"Hugo! How did it go, mate?" says Donald

"Gustavo no more!"

"Ya fucking dancer, Hugo. Did ye enjoy it?"

"To be honest mate I did, aye. He was on about killing the girls as well the dirty bastard."

"No way?"

"Yup."

Siham takes my extremely clean right hand and leads me upstairs.

"We need to phone Miss G," she said.

"That we do Siham."

Siham dials the number and then passes me the phone.

"Miss G, it's Hugo."

"Hello Hugo, how did it go?"

"It went fine, I'm sorry but I don't have any bullets left for you."

"Ah, good job indeed then?"

"Yes, that Gustavo was one nasty fucker."

"Yes, he was Hugo, now it's your time. I want you to clean this coast up now. No more LSD, Heroin and Acid. I want people to love each other and be chilled on this coast. As of tomorrow, we'll only deal in Cocaine, the best Hashish from Morocco, Ecstasy and Speed."

"Sounds good to me Miss G."

"Pepe will teach you everything and introduce you to contacts. The villa that you're in is now yours, I'll get you a brand new BMW dropped off tomorrow with a mobile phone and I'll also get you some credit cards. Is there anything else?"

"Yes, there is one thing. Siham - she wants to stay here with me and I'd like her too also."

"That's up to Siham, Hugo. I'll sort that out with Mustapha. Helima is a different story though, she'll need to leave in two days time as she has two children back in Morocco."

"Ok Miss G, I'll let everybody know."

"Tomorrow is a big day for you Hugo, you are now my second in command for southern Spain. Get some sleep, I have more surprises for you tomorrow. Good night."

"Night, Miss G."

I explain the news to Siham and we're both delighted. I don't know how I'm going to break the news to Donald the poor cunt will be heartbroken. I'll leave it till the morning cause I can hear him and Helima in that fucking jacuzzi again. She screams like a fucking banshee man.

CHAPTER TEN

CLEANING UP THE COAST

The girls wake us up with the smell of the breakfast cooking. Bacon can be smelled throughout the villa and it's fucking lovely. I'm looking forward to see what today brings but I'm not looking forward to telling Donald about Helima, but needs must.

"Morning boys"!

The two lassies look amazing and here's me and Donald in our hoosecoats and flip flops. Two Scottish Love Gods, right enough.

"Morning girls," Donald and I say, simultaneously

"Donald, I need to talk to you man."

"Whit's the craic, Hugo?"

"It's about Helima, mate. She has to go back to Morocco tomorrow pal, I'm sorry."

"Oh I know Hugo, she told me in the jacuzzi last night. I'm gutted, but it's only eight miles away from that La Linea place across the water."

"Ah, so you're awright then, man?"

"Aye, once we're up and running and the money is coming in, I can go and see her."

"Thank fuck for that mate, I was dreading telling you this morning."

"Naw it's fine Hugo, it's fine."

We chew the fat with the lassies over breakfast and I tell the group my plans. Pepe is coming for me in an hour and I'm taking Siham with me. Pepe wants to show me the business and introduce me to some contacts. Donald is taking Helima to Gibraltar for their last day together.

Pepe arrives in this brand new Black BMW and shouts me outside.

"Hugo! Come down here."

The four of us head outside to take a look at this motor.

"It's yours, Hugo, courtesy of Miss G."

I take a look inside. Leather seats, tinted windows and all the extras you need. There's a mobile phone in the middle as well with the longest lead known to man on it so you can talk from outside of the car if needs be.

"Wow! Man, this is fucking unreal. Pepe."

"Miss G has a lot of faith in you and wants to repay you. You did a good thing for her last night and she doesn't forget stuff like that. Enjoy it, it's yours."

Pepe comes inside whilst we all get sorted. Donald and Helima's taxi arrives to take them to Gibraltar. I arrange to pick them up at 10pm that night, as I'll just be over the border in La Linea. Today is the day that my life truly begins and I can't wait.

Pepe gathers me and Siham round the table. He pulls out a map of Southern Spain, lays it on the table and starts to explain my boundaries.

"Basically Hugo, from Estepona down the coast and all the way along to Tarifa is yours, including Gibraltar. The most important part that you control with an iron fist is the Straits of Gibraltar. It's the gateway from Africa to Europe and most of Europe's drugs come through the Straits."

"Wow, man, this is unreal."

"Stick to these boundaries Hugo and you'll be fine. Go out of them and there'll be hell to pay for all of us. Miss G has notified everybody that Gustavo is no longer with us and that you are now her second in command.

I'm going to take you to La Linea very soon because I have another surprise for you from Miss G. Ok, finally, the villa Here is the paperwork for the villa. Sign here and it's yours Hugo. I have tasked off an eight man, two shifts, 24 hour armed security team to protect you here. Two on the gate, four patrolling and two on rest at all times. You will be safe here."

"This is all insane Pepe, man it really is."

"Davie spoke very highly of you to Miss G and you have done nothing but fulfil your promises to her. She respects that and wants to show her gratitude to you that's all. Money is no problem to her; she is a billionairess and looks after those that look after her.

Oh, one last thing Hugo, the Mayor. He doesn't mess around in this province and as long as he gets paid, he's happy. He's got rid of big time Charlies' here before. The Peckham Four were here up until about 7 years ago and they got a bit big for their boots. They ran this coast until the Mayor found out they brought Cocaine here without his authority. They didn't listen. So he destroyed the;, cutting the head off one of the gang as a warning.

One of the other Peckham Four got gunned down by the Guardia Civil. A right bad bastard, named Sammy. Their leader, Charlie, is still supposed to be out here somewhere, but is still lying low. There was also some other kid, named Frankie, we think he fled back to England though Intelligence tells us that one day they hope to be back in business over here, so we'll just need to be ready for when that day comes."

"So, basically, keep the Mayor sweet; stay within our boundaries and clean up this coast as Miss G wishes?"

"Exactly Hugo, exactly. Do all these things and everybody will be happy."

"I'll certainly do as everyone wishes."

"Ok, let's get in the car and drive down to La Linea. I have one more surprise for you down there from Miss G - plus there's a few people waiting to meet you as well."

This has been one almighty rollercoaster this past week or so. I kinda don't want it to end. I've got myself a beautiful woman, a beautiful car and a beautiful Villa. I'm also running most of the Costa Del Sol drug trade now and have a Billionairess backing me. I don't know what else is in store for me but fuck me, I'm sure as hell looking forward to it.

CHAPTER ELEVEN

HUGO'S BAR AND GRILL

I get behind the wheel of my brand new BMW. Pepe sits in the front and Siham sits in the back.

"Where to, Pepe?"

"La Linea please, Hugo."

It was dark the last time we were there so I don't really know where I'm going, so Pepe directs me. The last time I was there as well, I got a bit of a doing so it's not the best place for me to be revisiting. The last time though, I was a tourist, now, I'm in charge."

We drive into La Linea and I remember the sign well. Petrol station on the left hand side and that fucking smell. Oaft!! There's a chicken factory as soon as you come in and it's fucking honking so it is. We keep driving in until we hit a roundabout, turn left and then head for the coast road towards Gibraltar.

As we're driving along the coast road in La Linea it's so impressive. There's local fishermen selling freshly caught seafood by the side of the road, but the one thing that really stands out is the majestic looking Rock of Gibraltar at the end of the road. It's stunning looking, it really is.

We go over a few speed bumps and across another roundabout and then Pepe asks me and Siham to keep an eye out on the buildings on the right hand side. There's little newsagents, butchers, hotels and Hugo's......

"Whit the fuck man, Pepe?"

"Turn back on ourselves Hugo at the next roundabout. Yes, you saw it right. Hugo's."

We turn round at the next roundabout and pull up outside this impressive looking bar. Sure enough the sign outside says Hugo's. The mobile phone goes off inside the car.

"Pick it up Hugo, it's your phone," says Pepe.

"Hello!"

"Hi,, Hugo it's Miss G here. This is your final surprise for now. I've had this Bar and Grill place completely converted for you in the past 48 hours, it's now your base here in La Linea. If you turn round now, I'm on my yacht on the Straits of Gibraltar, looking at you right now. I own these Straits and everything that comes through it.

Inside the bar are some people that I want you to meet. Mustapha. He is our Morocco contact and he will give us whatever we want from Morocco.

"Raslav. He is the head of the Russian Mafia in Puerto Banus and he wants to meet you too.

Bruno. He runs the 400 strong gang for you in La Linea with an iron fist. Enjoy your first meeting and enjoy your new bar.

There's one person missing who's in a crisis meeting just now. The Chief of the Local Police, Xavier Cortes. Xavier gets a monthly salary from you and it's triple his Police one so you won't get any problems from him."

"Miss G, I honestly don't know what to say. I'm flabbergasted by all of this."

"Enjoy it all and embrace it Hugo, this is your new life down here. Oh and one last piece of advice for now. Be ruthless in this meeting - put your marker down."

I take Siham's hand and we stroll into Hugo's. Pepe walks on in front and starts to walk up a spiral staircase. We follow him. The staircase takes us up to the roof terrace, where there's three men sat at a table. As I walk onto the terrace, the three men stand up. Pepe introduces me to them.

"Ok, Hugo, I'll take Siham down to the bar and leave you to your meeting. Jesus here will get you any Tapas or drinks that yourself or your guests need."

"No bother Pepe. Jesus, can I have a beer please and the same again for my guests?"

I take a quick look round the table. Mustapha is a skinny, dirty looking guy. Raslav is a big man, nae stranger to a fish supper that's for sure. Bruno looks like a heavyweight boxer, definitely somebody you wouldn't want a right/left combo from. I decide to just get right into it, no fucking about.

"Good afternoon Gents, I'm sure you've all heard about Gustavo already, so that should save me some time? Let me make one thing clear right away here. I don't fucking suffer fools gladly, so if you think that this might be the case, then please feel free to leave now."

Nobody moves an inch.

"Good, now let's get down to business. My plan is to totally change the drug scene down here and I've been told about my boundaries, which I'll happily keep to This town, for example is a fucking disgrace and with the help of everybody round this table, that'll change.

Bruno - Heroin, LSD and Acid will no longer be available from us from today. Hashish, Cocaine, Ecstasy and Speed only from now on. Tell your gang that if I find out anyone is caught selling anything other than those four drugs I've mentioned, it's their kneecaps.

If they still don't listen, they'll end up washing up off the Straits out there, I promise them.

Mustapha, whatever Gustavo ordered in Hashish from you, I want double it now. I want the South of Spain not only to be chilled, but I have connections in the UK and we'll get rid of it no bother. Again, Heroin is a no go on my Straits. Tell the dealers from everywhere else that they'll need to find another route to get it in from Afghanistan. "As of today, Southern Spain and Tangiers in Morocco won't be supplying it.

Finally, Raslav, I want to go into business with you reference Cocaine. I know you have contacts with the Colombians and Banus is the place to go for the best Coke. We don't have to fall out over being competitors, we can use the same supplier.

Oh, one last thing from me for now Bruno The people that attacked myself and my friend the other night. I want them all here at 11am tomorrow morning; I want to introduce myself. Also, I want to meet the gang members that will be working for me, have them all assemble at the Football stadium at 11.30am as well."

I wanted to get my point across to the guys and I think they got the message pretty loud and clear. After the frosty start, we started to have a laugh and get to know each other. Jesus got the Tapas and the beer flowing and we started to really enjoy each others company. I instructed Jesus to invite Siham and Pepe up to the roof and we took in the amazing views.

I totally forgot I was meant to pick up Donald and Helima from Gibraltar at 10pm to head back to the Villa. Myself and Siham have had a few too many refreshments, so I slip Jesus a few Pesetas to pick them up and drive us all back.

I tell Donald all about my day and tell him my plans for our twenty or so attackers in the morning. He just laughs and says I'm mental. I feel for him tonight because his Lady is going home tomorrow. I haven't seen him this happy before.

CHAPTER TWELVE

UNTIL WE MEET AGAIN

The housekeeper bounces into the villa again slamming the fucking front doors. That'll be every cunt up then, eh? This is the day that a few heads are going to roll. I don't mind a square go, but twenty odd against two is a fucking liberty man. Regardless if you're following instructions.

I can hear that jacuzzi on. It's 8am ffs. I put a towel on and look over the balcony. Now I'm a heartless bastard, but the sight of Donald and Helima cuddling in that Jacuzzi is a cracking sight to waken up to. The poor cunt is going to be lost when she goes. I'll need to keep him busy for the next few days and take his mind off things.

As I walk back into the room, Siham turns round and looks at me. Thank God she's going nowhere. Utter perfection staring right at me. One lucky guy! We get a shower and head down for our last breakfast with Helima.

Siham walks on in front and my belly is rumbling like fuck with all that Tapas and beer yesterday. Helima passes me on the way back from the jacuzzi and Donald starts to walk up the stairs. He's about 10 metres away from me so I decide to crop dust the bastard.

I let oot this fart and it's fucking stinking, man. I keep on walking down the stairs and he's walking up them and BANG!! Perfect.

"Morning, Hugo!!"

Donald cops the fucking lot in his gub hahahahaha.

"Ya fucking dirty bastard, Hugo, that's fucking rotten man."

Job done!!

"That's for me no' being able to go in that jacuzzi ya dirty cunt. You want me to swallow your spunk but you'll no' swallow a wee fart?"

"A wee fart? My fucking eyebrows are slipping aff with that wan, fur fuck sake."

The two love birds come back doon the stairs. Donald's eyebrows are intact and we enjoy our last breakfast with Helima. The next hour is filled with Siham and Helima greeting then Donald gets her bags from the room.

Myself and Siham say our goodbyes and leave the two of them to it. Donald puts Helima in her Taxi and stands there at the front door until it's out of sight.

"Until we meet again Helima!!" The poor cunt shouts.

I'll take the poor fucker to La Linea with me today and cheer him up. Jesus will be back for us soon to take us to Hugo's. Bruno better have around twenty odd folk waiting there for me.

Jesus turns up at 10.20am to take us to La Linea. I give Siham some Pesetas to go to Marbella to get herself some nice clothes and get her hair done. We then take the wee drive down the coast to La Linea. As we arrive at Hugo's there's a crowd of around twenty outside. When Jesus opens my door and me and Donald step outside, their faces are a fucking picture.

"Ok, Bruno, get everyone up to the roof terrace, I need a chat with everyone."

The twenty or so sheepishly go up to the roof under Bruno's command then me and Donald follow them up.

"Bruno, I'd like you to translate the following please my good man."

"No problem boss."

"As of yesterday, La Linea and their surrounding towns and cities from Tarifa all the way to Estepona belong to me."

Bruno starts to translate.

"Just over a week ago, Gustavo ordered you all to attack myself and my friend here over a drug debt which you all did. Between you all, you now owe me £5000 which I will take out of your wages in Pesetas. Bruno will give you all jobs to do until you have paid me back.

About the assault now. I'd fight and kick the living fuck out of the twenty of you right now, but you're going to experience what myself and friend experienced. Bruno, walk the twenty of them to the football stadium and I'll get you there in 15 mins."

Bruno and a few of his boys shepherd the junkies down to the local football stadium while me and Donald head downstairs for a quick beer.

"What you doing giving them a job Hugo? They kicked oor cunts in?"

"Hopefully if they're working, it'll help them get aff the gear."

Me and Donald have a wee Beer then get Jesus to drive us down to the stadium. As we approach, Bruno is waiting outside to greet us.

"Boss, everybody is here. We have a microphone rigged up for you. There's 400 of the local gang here, plus those 20 that attacked yourself and your friend."

"Good job Bruno, have the 20 stand in the centre circle and I want the 400 to line the football pitch please all the way round. I'll tell you what I want to say to them all and you speak on the microphone explaining my instructions."

"No problem, Hugo."

The 20 herd themselves in the centre circle and the local gang cover the outer lining of the pitch.

"Start translating Bruno.

Good afternoon Ladies and Gentlemen "My name is Hugo and this is my friend Donald. A few days ago I assassinated Gustavo and I'm now your new boss. Those twenty people in the centre circle assaulted myself and my friend, under the command of Gustavo. There were only two of us against all of them so it didn't end well for us.

Now they are surrounded by 400 people that work for me and it doesn't look good for them. I'm a fair guy, but I'm also a fucking ruthless one. If any of you in this stadium cross me, I'll be firm but fair. Addiction and greed cost these twenty individuals to do what they did that night.

I've decided to give them jobs to do to pay back the £5000 they decided to steal from me to pay for their addiction. So, here's what's going to happen. Everybody in the centre circle take your tops off.

What you did that night was a fucking liberty and I won't tolerate that. Let the next two minutes be a lesson to you all. Everybody turn round and face the centre circle. I don't want anybody killed here, but for the next two minutes, everybody kick the living fuck out of these twenty. Go!!"

The 400 strong run towards the helpless 20 and give them a right good doing. I had to send the message out that I wasn't to be messed with and this was the best way to do it. I took no pleasure in watching the beating but it had to be done. After two minutes, I give the order for the pack to stop and return to where they were.

I survey the centre circle and everyone is at least moving but down.

"As I said, let that be a lesson to everyone. I'm nothing like Gustavo, so let's clean this coast up together. No more Heroin on this coast, because it has ruined it. We're going into the Cocaine game and teaming up with the Russians from Banus. I want a better clientele coming to this end of the coast.

With Cocaine comes money for everybody. As of today, everybody will get a 10% wage rise from what Gustavo was paying you. You've just shown me your immediate loyalty, so I'll reward that. Those people in the centre circle are no longer your enemies, but your co-workers, so everybody get in there and help them to their feet and clean them up."

The local gang walk this time, instead of running towards the centre circle, and start to help the unfortunate twenty. I think I got my message across to everyone. I gave the local gang a wage rise and gained a huge amount of respect for Bruno. He didn't let me down today and I appreciate that.

I get Donald and Bruno to come back to Hugo's with me and as we're driving along the coast, Donald pipes up.

"Would you look at that, Hugo."

"Look at whit Donald?"

"Morocco Hugo, Morocco. It's beautiful over there. Helima, I miss her."

CHAPTER THIRTEEN

MOROCCO

The next few weeks go off incident free and business is good. Bruno is running things nicely in La Linea and I've kept an eye on the Straits, from my bar on the shore front. We've eradicated the Heroin problem on the coast, but our European contacts aren't happy that the Straits aren't allowed now as a way in. Tough fucking titty really.

Gibraltar is really booming at the minute with high rise buildings going up everywhere and lots of gaming companies coming in. Their workers love the Charlie, so we're making a fortune there. It's tempting to expand up the coast and beyond, but those Russians in Banus are mental. That's at least twenty murdered in the last few weeks that've crossed them.

I'm worried about Donald, since Helima has gone, he's went back to becoming a right boring bastard again and he's starting to get on my tits now, to be honest. I think I'll have a chat with him.

"Donald, you need to fucking start getting a grip, man."

"What do you mean, Hugo?"

"Since Helima went you've gone right back into your shell again. I've made a decision. You've got two choices here. I either give you a wedge and you go back to Scotland, or I give you a wedge and you fuck off to Morocco and work with Mustapha and then you'll get to see Helima? Make your decision Donald and get back to me, because you're no use to me here, like this."

"Hugo, I appreciate what you've done for me and that but this isn't for me this lifestyle man. I'm scared to be honest. I've just got a bad feeling about all of this. I think I'll go and see Helima one last time and then head back to Scotland."

"Right, I'm sorry mate I really am. I know this isn't for you and you've stuck it out longer than I expected but it's time to move on. I tell you what, Siham is missing Helima too. Why don't the three of us go over for a few days, eh? I'll get Pepe and Bruno to cover things here for a few days and I'll square it away with Miss G. I could do with a few days away anyway."

"Aye, that'd be nice Hugo. A wee farewell weekend in Tangiers."

I phone Miss G and ask for a few days off. She's fine with the whole situation. I then tell Siham the good news about a wee trip back to Morocco to see Helima and she's absolutely buzzing. Pepe and Bruno are briefed up to keep an eye on things until my return. The three of us are buzzing. Morocco here we come.

Bruno sorts out a powerful rib for us and a driver and we leave La Linea and head the 8 miles to across the straits of Gibraltar to Morocco. To see Siham's face light up as we approach her Country is a sight to behold. I'm thinking of proposing to her on this trip. She's unbelievable.

We get off the boat and Mustapha is waiting for us and drops us off at a luxury hotel in the centre. Helima is waiting for us at the main door and Donald starts to lighten up once again. I feel bad about sending him home but this line of work just isn't for him.

Siham and Helima don't want to let each other go either. Maybe this wee weekend away was a masterstroke. We put our stuff in the rooms and head out into the City. Helima and Siham want to show us a good time. We hit a few bars and clubs and have an excellent wee night.

My plan tomorrow is to go a wee walk with Donald in the City and buy her a ring. I'll propose on the last night. The lassies want to keep drinking when we get back to the hotel, so we leave them to it. They haven't seen each other for a wee while.

I wake up at 8am and Siham isn't anywhere to be seen. I bang Donald's door and when he opens, there's no sign of Helima either.

> "Where the fuck ur they two, fur fucks sake?" says Hugo

The boys get changed quickly and run down to the Hotel bar. The two girls are still there drinking.

> "Whit the fucks going here Siham?" says Hugo

> "What? We're best friends, Hugo. We've missed each other and just catching up."

The two of them can hardly stand let alone talk. We take them upstairs, help them out their shoes and just put them into the same bed to sleep it off. I grab a towel and head into Donald's room with him.

> "Right, I want to get her a ring Donald. I'm gonna propose to her tonight."

> "No fucking way man, you serious?"

> "Course I'm serious, I'm in love with her. Let's get a shower and boost into town. We'll grab breakfast and we'll have a few beers. Give them four or five hours kip to sleep that off."

> "Sounds good to me, pal."

We head into town and get the ring first before we get pished. We decide to forget the food and just get straight into the beer. It's flowing nicely so the five hours turns into eight then we decide to head back. They can hardly complain after their antics last night. I'll need to get a shower and square myself up for the big proposal.

As we turn round the corner towards the hotel, there's five Polis motors and two Ambulances outside. As we approach the first Ambulance there's nobody in it, but Helima is sitting in the 2nd one.

"What the fuck has happened, Helima?" shouts Donald

"It's Siham!!"

Helima then goes into hysterics.

"Siham, my beautiful Siham!" she screams

"Righ,t Helima, calm down here, where's Siham?" asks Hugo

"She's dead, Hugo, she's dead!!"

"What the fuck do you mean she's fucking dead?"

"I woke up to this horrible smell, Siham must've vomited in her sleep and choked on it. She's gone Hugo!!"

Hugo sinks to his knees and puts his hands over his face.

"FUCKING NOOOOOOOOOOOOOO!!"! "Where is she now?"

"She's still in the room, Hugo, the Police are checking the scene."

Hugo gets up off his knees and marches straight up to the room. As he comes out of the lift he's met by a wall of Police. They say something to him in Arabic, but he has no clue what.

"Let me fucking past, ya cun,t or I'll burst ye!!"

They start to restrain him until one of them who speaks English starts to talk to him.

"Sir, where is it you're trying to go? This floor is closed for now."

"Room 1967, that's my Lady in that room. I've just been told what's happened. Let me see her, for God's sake."

"We can't let you see her. It's a crime scene, Sir, until we've cleared it otherwise."

The smell coming down the corridor is stomach curdling. God knows how long she's been lying in her own vomit. Hugo can only stand there and stare at the door where his only ever love is lying in a bed covered in her own vomit, dead. He's helpless.

After two more hours, they finally bring her body out and wheel it past him.

"Stop. Stop, stop!!" he shouts.

The Coroner's stop the trolley and let Hugo put his hands on Siham through the plastic sheet covering, for one last time. He breaks down in uncontrollable tears. Tears filled with sadness and with anger.

"Why did I fucking leave you Siham?" he shouts

A Policeman puts his hand on Hugo's shoulder to comfort him and the Coroner's wheel the trolley with Siham's body on it, into the lift accompanied by two Police officers. All the Police tape is pulled away and Hugo is free to go back into the room.

He walks into the bedroom and stands there and just stares at the bed. He stands there for what must be about thirty minute,s with tears streaming down his face. He then flips the bed and wrecks the entire room. He sits there sobbing uncontrollably again. Donald and Helima walk in.

"Hugo mate, we're sorry, we really are."

Hugo just looks up at Donald through his blurry, puffy and teary eyes and just nods. The next hour or so, Helima and Donald start to tidy up the room that Hugo's wrecked. It's a tense time so Donald and Helima go next door and give him some space. The next morning, Donald chaps Hugo's door at 9am.

"Hugo, Hugo pal, you there?"

"Aye, Donald, give me a minute."

Hugo comes to the door.

"Donald, I will never touch a drop of alcohol ever again in my life. That's what's caused all of this."

"Hugo, mate, don't blame anything, it was a complete accident."

Helima then walks into the room.

"Hugo, we need to go and collect Siham and prepare her body for an Islamic funeral. She has to be buried within 24 hours. We will take her to a funeral home and prepare her for which I have arranged already."

"Prepare her?" asks Hugo

"Yes, Hugo, prepare her."

CHAPTER FOURTEEN

GOODBYE MY BEAUTIFUL SIHAM

I contact Miss G and the boys in La Linea and explain the situation. Miss G tells me to take as long as I need. Now, I've only had to bury my parents before and that was pretty straight forward back in Scotland. Thank God Helima is here though, or I'd be fucked. An Islamic Funeral? What the fuck is that? I guess I'm about to get a crash course in one.

We meet the people from the funeral home at the hospital and they collect Siham. We then drive to funeral home and they wheel my precious Siham inside. After ten minutes we get shown into this well lit room and there she is, under a white sheet, on a trolley. My beautiful Siham. She looks so much at peace and I move her hair away from her face and kiss her freezing cold forehead.

"Ok, Hugo, we need to prepare her body for burial,." says Helima

Donald steps outside and it's just myself, Helima and Siham left inside. Helima is carrying lots of white garments and stuff to wash Siham with. She's brought a hairbrush and lots of other stuff. I'm not sure what's about to happen here.

"Ok, Hugo, to prepare the body for burial, it must be washed and shrouded. It's normally close, same-sex family members that are encouraged to give Ghusl, though in Siham's case, she doesn't have any family, so we will do it.

Her body needs to be washed three times. If, after three washings, the body is not entirely clean, it may be washed more, though ultimately the body should be washed an odd number of times.

Her body should be washed in the following order: upper right side, upper left side, lower right side, lower left side.

Siham's hair will then be washed and braided into three braids "Once clean and prepared, her body should be covered in a white sheet.

To shroud her body, three large white sheets of inexpensive material, that I have here, should be laid on top of each other. Her body should be placed on top of the sheets.

Siham will then be dressed in an ankle-length, sleeveless, dress and head veil which I've brought with me too.

Then, Siham's left hand should rest on her chest and the right hand should rest on the left hand, as in a position of prayer.

The sheets should then be folded over her body, first the right side and then the left side, until all three sheets have wrapped her body.

The shrouding should be secured with ropes, one tied above the head, two tied around her body, and one tied below the feet.

Her body will then be transported to the mosque for funeral prayers, known as Salat al-Janazah.

Once all of this is done, we can bury her, Hugo. Does this all make sense?"

"Not really Helima, not to me, but I trust you. Thank you for everything, I don't know what I would've done without you."

We start preparing Siham's body and Helima talks me through everything again, step by step. I keep stopping and breaking my heart because I know that this will be the last time I ever see Siham. I meticulously clean her body three times with Helima and then we finish off the other tasks.

The guys at the funeral home then transport her to the local Mosque, just across the street, for the start of the funeral service. When we get there, there's about forty local people already inside praying. We take our shoes and socks off and they welcome us in with open arms.

"Whit's going to happen now, Helima?" asks Hugo

"I'll explain now, Hugo. Salat al-Janazah (funeral prayers) should be performed by all members of the community. Though the prayers should be recited at the Mosque, they should not be recited inside the Mosque; instead, they should be performed in a prayer room or study room, or in the Mosque's courtyard. Those praying should face the "qiblah"—that is, toward Mecca—and form at least three lines, with the male most closely related to the person who died in the first line, followed by men, then children, then women."

"So, I've to go to the front then Helima?" asks Hugo

"Yes of course, you and Donald. She had nobody else, don't worry, I'll be at the back."

Me and Donald just stand there will our heads bowed as we have absolutely no clue what's being said. It was quite amazing actually how this wee community did this for her, in such a short space of time but I suppose they're used to it. There's no way we could everybody back home together as quickly to bury someone within 24 hours.

Once the prayers are over, the men carry Siham down the street and all the local people come out of their houses to pay their respects. They carry her about 100 metres to the cemetery. I ask Helima what's about to happen now.

"After Salat al-Janazah has been recited, the body should be transported to the cemetery. Traditionally, Hugo, only men are allowed to be present at the burial, though in some communities all mourners, including women, will be allowed at the gravesite.

The grave has been dug perpendicular to the qiblah, and her body will be placed in the grave on its right side, facing the qiblah. Those placing her body into the grave should recite the line "Bismilllah wa ala millati rasulilllah" ("In the name of Allah and in the faith of the Messenger of Allah").

Once her body is in the grave, a layer of wood or stones should be placed on top of her body to prevent direct contact between her body and the soil that will fill the grave. Then each mourner present will place three handfuls of soil into the grave.

Once the grave has been filled, a small stone or marker may be placed at the grave so that it is recognisable. However, traditionally, it is prohibited to erect a large monument on the grave or decorate the grave in an elaborate way."

We arrive at the graveside an all of what Helima said took place. I just stood there and watched it all take place. Helima was allowed to stand beside me - as they aren't as strict in Northern Morocco as they are in other parts of Africa - and she held my hand tightly. It was a horrible day but lovely the way the Morroccan's dealt with my beautiful Siham.

I approached her grave to put my three handfuls of soil in and just uttered these simple words.

"Goodbye, my beautiful Siham."

I looked at her one last time and as the tears ran down my face, a smile appeared too as I was just glad to have had her in my life for this short space of time. In my last handful of soil was the engagement ring I bought her and as I threw it in my heart just sank. I don't think I will ever love again after this. My heart is completely broken.

We say our goodbyes to the locals and head back to the Hotel. Donald is heading back to Scotland in the morning, so I decide to leave him and Helima alone. I need to get back to Spain before I crack up, so I phone Mustapha to get me a rib sorted, to get me across the Straits.

Helima has been a rock today so I leave her the remaining suitcase of money I have for her and her young family. I thank her from the bottom of my heart and give Donald a handshake. My driver has arrived to take me to the Port. Spain here I come.

CHAPTER FIFTEEN

HOSPITAL RESCUE

As we're hurtling across the Straits of Gibraltar in the rib, I can't help but just stare at the Rock and think of Siham. It really is a majestic sight during the day but at night under the moon it's just spectacular. We pull into La Linea and Bruno and Pepe are waiting for me with a car.

"Hugo my friend, I'm so sorry to hear about Siham", says Pepe.

"Me too, Hugo," says Bruno.

"If there's anything either of us can do Hugo then please don't hesitate to ask" says Pepe.

"Thanks lads, has everything been ok since I've been away?"

"We have a bit of a crisis to be honest Hugo, but wanted to take you home to get some rest and then we were going to tell you all about it in the morning," says Bruno.

"Well, what sort of fucking crisis Bruno?"

"We had some smugglers get chased on a rib from Morocco today. We lost a lot of Hashish, Hugo. The Guardia Civil managed to catch one of them and he's under armed guard in La Linea Hospital. They ran him over when he tried to flee on a moped. He's alive, with broken bones, but under guard in Casualty."

"Right, Bruno, drive me to the bar."

We pull up to Hugo's and the place is jumping with guys from the local gang. I instruct Bruno to get everybody off the roof terrace and downstairs into the bar. I walk in after Pepe and shut the doors.

"Bruno, translate this for me. We have one of our smugglers in the local hospital. The local Police can't do anything, as he's under armed guard by the Guardia Civil. I want everybody to go home and get a balaclava and get their arses back here in half an hour. Go!!"

The twenty or so gang members that are in the bar leave straight away. Pepe just gives me a look of confusion as to what I'm up to. There's only me, Jesus, Pepe, Bruno and a few local hookers left in the bar.

"What's the plan, boss?" asks Bruno

"We're going to fucking rescue him, that's the fucking plan Bruno."

"Are you mad boss?"

"Yer fucking right I am!!"

I start to look around the bar. Is this what I really want now with Siham not here? I have sex on tap if I want it with the local hookers, but I'm not interested. Jesus gets me a beer, but I refuse and explain that I no longer drink.

"Are you sure this is a good idea boss? We could have the whole of the Guardia Civil or even the Army here in the morning because of this," says Pepe.

"Fuck them all Pepe. I run this coast and I'm about to show them why."

The gang start to arrive back at the bar in dribs and drabs.

"Get me a balaclava from the store room, Bruno," says Hugo

"Boss, come on."

"Fucking move yer arse."

"Ok boss."

Everybody is back and I gather them all on the roof so the hookers don't hear the plan. I know for a fact they don't just fuck the local gang. They fuck coppers as well, who bribe them. Bruno, as ever, is by my side to translate.

"One of our drug smugglers is under armed guard in the local hospital and we're going to rescue him. We're going to use the element of surprise as they won't be expecting this. Bruno has informed me that he's under surveillance in the Casualty dept and when we get there, one of the Porters is going to lead us straight to the cubicle.

There's five, 4x4 Land Cruisers outside, so we'll use them. We'll park up outside the hospital, once we see the porter - and on my command - we'll rush the Casualty department mob handed. Straight into the cubicle, detain the officers and handcuff them to the bed. We'll relieve them of their keys and their guns.

No shots will be fired by us and no violence either. Straight in and straight out, with the smuggler. Bruno will take the smuggler in his car to a safe house up the coast until all of this blows over. Does anybody have any questions?"

Nobody puts their hand up.

"Good, everybody get in a car."

The hospital is less than a mile away and we drive in convoy under the cover of darkness and park up right outside the hospital. The young Porter comes outside and approaches Bruno's car. Bruno gives me the thumbs up in the car behind, so I get out. As I get out the car, the twenty strong local gang follow my lead and we storm the Hospital.

We go straight in through the front doors, right into the middle of the casualty dept. Not one person screams or utters a word because every single person in that Hospital knows exactly what's about to happen now except the two Guardia Civil officers in cubicle four.

I'm right at the front with Bruno and open the cubicle curtain. I grab one officer and Bruno grabs the other. Then about five guys each take over and hold the officers down and then handcuff them to the bed. Four guys grab the smuggler and carry him out and straight into Bruno's 4x4. Job done.

We all depart the Hospital, go our separate ways and my 4x4 heads back to the bar. I instruct Jesus to take the balaclavas from my car outside the back and burn them. It's not long before the sirens can be heard. It's also not long before the Local chief of Police arrives at my bar.

"I'm looking for Hugo," says the man in the Local Police uniform to Jesus.

Jesus points to my table where I'm sat with Pepe.

"Hugo, my name is Xavier Cortes, we haven't met yet, but I assume Miss G has told you about me."

"Ah, yes,, Xavi, she did mention you but said you were at some sort of crisis meeting I believe?"

"That is correct, Hugo, yes. You pulled off a daring move tonight rescuing your boy."

"I don't know what you mean, Xavi."

"Listen Hugo, let's not go around the houses here. The Mayor is just off the phone to me and he's not fucking happy Your only saving grace is that those two officers weren't injured or there'd be hell to pay tonight. We don't like the Guardia Civil sticking their noses into our business here so well done."

"Thanks Xavi." Now, can I get you anything?"

"A beer and two of those girls over there, please, Hugo."

I motion Jesus to get Xavi a beer and bring two girls over to the table for him. It looks like my plan just to handcuff the officers was a masterstroke, or this place would be swarming. We got a result tonight, but it coud've been much different. I ply Xavi with booze and leave him with Jesus and the girls.

I get Pepe to drive me back to the Villa up the coast. It's been a mad couple of days. I need to get some good kip and decide what I'm going to do with my life now. Head back to Scotland or continue this mental lifestyle down here?

CHAPTER SIXTEEN

GUARDIA CIVIL PAYBACK

The next few weeks pass off without incident and business is booming again. I've got the tobacco smugglers doing well in Gibraltar. The gaming company employees are sniffing more and more cocaine as well. We've upgraded the engines on our ribs so Customs and the Cops have no chance of catching them coming back from Morocco. Life is good.

The problem though in life is that when everything is going well, something or somebody, comes along and boots you right in the balls.

I'm in the bar with Bruno and a few of the boys when the phone goes.

"Hugo, it's for you," says Jesus.

"Hello!"

"Hello Hugo, it's Donald here, how are you doing?"

"Donald, whit a surprise ma. Whit's happening?"

"It's bad news I'm afraid Hugo but just wanted to let you know. Auld Sadie from the pub died yesterday morning. Wan of the new lassies that started in there, "Mel", found her when she went in for her shift. The poor lassie was in a right state."

"Aw fur fuck sake, man"!

"That's not all Hugo. Auld Roberto that retired from the bookies died the other day too. The toon is in shock. Both their funerals are next week. Will you be able to get back fur them, Hugo?"

"I'll definitely try mate, thanks for letting me know."

"Ok Hugo, look after yourself."

"Aye."

I head back to the table.

"Everything ok boss?" asks Bruno

"Ah just a bit of bad news from home pal. A couple of old people that I knew from my toon have just died."

"I'm sorry to hear that Hugo."

"Ah, it's fine."

We sit down and discuss local business and sort the months pay out for our workers when all of a sudden, two gang members burst into the pub covered in blood.

"What the fuck!!"

Bruno runs over with me and asks them something in Spanish.

"What are they saying Bruno?"

"They got dragged out of their car and driven away by the Guardia Civil. They got beaten up by four officers and got told that there's plenty more where that's coming from. Then they were dropped back off at the La Linea border."

"Ohhhhhhhhh fucking really?"

The next few weeks see more and more of my dealers and prostitutes being abducted off the streets by them and beaten, but the final straw came when they took two 18 year old boys up to the hills in Mijas, shot them in the legs and the poor boys had to leopard crawl for two miles to the nearest village. No fucking more!!

I didn't want to get into a full scale war with the Guardia Civil as there would only be one winner, but I had to do something. I needed a plan so I summoned all the local prostitutes to the bar. Bruno translates as usual.

"Ladies welcome! Now, don't panic, you're not in any trouble here. The Guardia Civil have been a little heavy handed with us all recently, due to the incident at the hospital and us embarrassing them. I want to put an end to it all, enough is enough. Now, I know you fuck them as well as other coppers, money is money. I want to know what they get up to off duty. Any ideas?"

One of the prostitutes puts her hand up. Her English is perfect.

"I know that every Sunday, they all meet up in a Cafe in El Rinconcillo, which isn't too far away from here, on the outskirts of Algeciras It's the rapid response unit that deal with the drug trade here as well. They're the bastards that have been attacking us all and shot those poor boys."

"Really? Thank you for that information. You stay behind so I can repay you for your intel."

I dismiss the other hookers, give the prostitute who provided the information a wedge of Pesetas and give her the night off. I then sit and start to devise a plan that'll put an end to all of this.

I decide to recce the cafe first thing tomorrow (Saturday) with Pepe and Bruno and three prostitutes, so we look like three ordinary couples. I let Jesus know that I want three girls here at 10am and retire back to my villa for the night.

I get up around 9am and after a shower, drive down the coast to Hugo's in La Linea. As I walk in, there are three girls sat there alongside Pepe and Bruno. I decide that we drive to the Cafe in three seperate cars so it looks like we're all meeting up as friends. We set off from Hugo's in five minute intervals and the girls direct us to the Guardia Civils meet up point.

When the three seperate cars arrive, we sit at a big table and take in the scenery. I can see why they come here, it's beautiful and out the way. I come up with a wee plan.

"Bruno, explain to the waitress that you've just been promoted to the rapid response squad and you've to meet your new colleagues here tomorrow, but not sure of what time "Explain that you don't know what they look like and wondered where they normally sit, so you don't look silly."

Bruno calls the waitress over and she's only too happy to help. She points out the table situated round the corner away from prying eyes, but outside. It has two entrances and exits by road, so perfect for an ambush. We can flank them from either side. Like their colleagues in the hospital, the daft bastards won't expect this one.

We head back to La Linea and I draw up a makeshift Map and summon a forty strong gang to the bar via Bruno. The waitress told Bruno that they meet at 11am, every single Sunday. I get Pepe to acquire me forty sub-machine guns. I want to put the fear of God into these cunts. I instruct Bruno to get me eight, 4x4 Land cruisers as well, to transport us all.

Back at the bar, I go through the plan with the forty strong gang, so that everybody knows to a tee what we're doing. I summon everybody to meet back here at 10am the next morning to put the plan into action. The Land Cruisers are ready, the guns are ready and we set off for the Cafe next morning.

As we approach the road before the cafe, four cars tail off to come up the hill to the side of the cafe and the other four tail off to come down it. The plan is to arrive outside the cafe at exactly the same time and ambush them. Again, no killing or violence, just a very strong warning. If they don't listen, the next time I won't be so lenient.

Bruno is in the lead car with me at the top of the hill, each car has walkie talkies. I give the instruction.

"Vamos, Vamos Vamos!!"

Everybody pulls their balaclavas down, we hurtle towards the cafe and come to a screeching halt outside it. The forty strong gang of us get out our vehicles and point our sub-machine guns directly at the nine off duty Guardia Civil rapid response guys and I gave Bruno a message to give to them.

"Listen in and take this warning very seriously. We not only know where you hang out, we know where you live, where your kids go to school and your exact movements. If another person belonging to our organisation, from Tarifa to Estepona, is harmed again, we will wipe each and every one of you and your families out. Make no mistake about that!!

Also, if this incident gets reported up the chain of command, then expect the full wrath of what I've just explained to you. Keep out of our way and we'll keep out of yours. I hope this message gets across to you all loud and clear. The next time, the forty of us will riddle you all with bullets."

We get back into our cars and head back to La Linea - jubilant. Those cunts know that we'll annihilate them now if they come after us. We've found their hideout and the fact that they were helpless is a huge victory for us.

The gang all head back to the bar and party with the girls. Siham is still very much on my mind so I head back to the villa. I have a meeting with Mustapha in Gibraltar tomorrow, so I'm going to turn in so that I'm fresh for it. Today was a good day, a moral victory.

CHAPTER SEVENTEEN

GIBRALTAR

Now, barring Edinburgh Castle, I don't think there's a more beautiful site than when you first see the Rock of Gibraltar. It's just majestic. If you step out of Hugo's and look right, you can see it at the end of La Linea and it's simply stunning. I'm meeting Mustapha there this morning and I can't wait.

As I get to the border, Guardia Civil officers are there and they know exactly who I am. I get a nod from them as I go through passport control. It's a fifteen to twenty minute walk from the border into the main Casemates Square. I'm meeting Mustapha in a wee bar named, "The Horseshoe Bar", on Main Street, which is just a five minute walk from the main square.

As I approach, Mustapha is already there on the one of the tables outside and he has a lady with him with jet black hair. She turns around and it's Helima, I can't believe it. I give Helima a massive hug and shake Mustapha's hand.

"I can't believe this Helima, how are you? What an excellent surprise!"

"I'm fine Hugo, I asked Mustapha if I could come along for this trip."

"Well I'm glad you did. Have you been to see Siham?"

"Yes Hugo, every day."

"I never really got the chance to say it in Morocco, but I couldn't have coped without you over there, Helima, so thank you so much from the bottom of my heart."

"It's no problem Hugo, it really wasn't. She was like my sister."

Mustapha stands up.

"First of all Hugo, let me give you my deepest condolences about Siham. She was a lovely woman."

"Yes, she was Mustapa. Yes, she was."

"Hugo, I have some bad news for you my friend. As you know, 70% of all the Hashish that comes to Europe, comes through Morocco and your Straits of Gibraltar. Customs and the Police have upped their game recently and we keep losing ribs." "We need to upgrade our boats Hugo because we're losing too much."

"Ok, Mustapha, well we will. Bigger engines and more skilled drivers is the answer."

"Exactly Hugo, that's why I've brought you to this bar. This an old Navy bar, we can recruit in here. We can offer these guys £50,000 a trip if it gets through and there's no better drivers of ribs than these Navy lads. They're highly skilled at huge speeds. Get some of your tobacco smugglers and prostitutes to drink here and start recruiting."

"Great idea Mustapha. I'll get Miss G to order us more powerful engines and better ribs for our smugglers. We need to spend money to make money. I'll also see about getting us a coupe of military grade radars and get them put into a couple of our safe houses in La Linea."

"Excellent idea Hugo, excellent."

We chat away for the next couple of hours, have a spot of lunch and then it's time to leave. I was gutted to leave Helima behind. I can see why Donald fell for her as much as I fell for Siham. She told me that they won't see each other again and she's told him that. Poor guy.

As I'm walking back down Main Street, I see this guy stumbling about and as I get closer he's got a Scotland top on. He looks pished out of his face.

"Here pal, you ok?" I ask

"Aye pal, I'm jist fucking steaming mate. Ahm I heading towards La Linea this way?"

"Naw, mate yer no. Yer going in the opposite direction. Come w'i me man, I'm going that way anyway."

"Aw cheers pal."

The poor cunt is oot his box on drink. He's no harming anybody, but if I don't get him over the border then he's going to get lifted. I ask him his name and he says it's Kris. I get him a taxi to the border and then a taxi to his address which took about half an hour to get out of him. I slip a card for Hugo's in his pocket and make sure he gets home ok.

I head back to Hugo's because I need to phone Miss G. The usual crowd are in and Jesus pours my now new preferred drink of choice, white coffee. I go through the back office to phone the boss.

"Hello."

"Miss G, it's Hugo."

"Hugo, I see you've been busy and hitting the headlines recently with the hospital raid etc?"

"Aye, we had to get the boy out."

"See that's why I like you Hugo, no shots fired and nobody harmed. Gustavo would've killed those officers and we'd be fucked You're a thinker and I like that." "What can I do for you Hugo?"

"Customs and the Police are seizing more and more of our stuff now from Morocco Miss G. We can't get away from their high powered boats anymore. We need bigger and faster boats."

"I'll speak to Pepe and get that sorted, right away Hugo. Anything else for you?"

"No, no, everything is going fine Ma'am. Everybody is getting paid, the Guardia Civil don't come near us now and barring this blip with some seizures, business is good."

"Good Hugo, glad to hear it. Keep up the good work!"

I head back into the bar and it's busy again. The place is booming and it's definitely the place to go. No trouble, good music and plenty of women. I stay out tonight as it's a good atmosphere. It approaches 3am and I see this boy walk in that I recognise at the bar. It's that young guy, Kris, from earlier on this afternoon in Gibraltar.

"Kris!"

"Eh, aye, hello."

"I'm looking for the owner. Was a in here earlier? I woke up with this caird for "Hugo's" in my pocket and just wanted to come in and apologise mate if I was a dick or that?"

"Naw son, ye wurnae in here. I met you in Gibraltar earlier. Ye were steaming so I got you a taxi hame and helped you into yer flat. I put a caird in yer pocket so you'd come in and I'd know ye were ok. My girlfriend choked on her vomit after drinking and died, so it puts the fear of shite up me"

"Aw I'm sorry to hear that man. I'm Kris Little mate."

"Hugo."

I shake the boys hand and get Jesus to get him a Beer.

"Wait a minute son, Kris Little?"

"Aye, how?"

"Davie's nephew?"

"Aye, how do you know Davie."?

"How do I know Davie haha? Well fuck me sideways."

I sit doon with young Kris and chat away about how I know his uncle Davie and how it was him that sent me here in the first place. Kris explains that he works for the biggest Bank in Gibraltar, but doesn't like it and is heading back to Scotland at the end of the month.

As he starts to top himself up with the drink, he starts to reveal a few of the Bank's security secrets. Could this be an option? A bank job of all bank jobs? I could get out of this business for good and set myself up for life here.

CHAPTER EIGHTEEN

TROUBLE IN SCOTLAND

Young Kris starts to become a regular in my bar now. Probably because I give him free bevvy. There's a method behind my madness though. Like I said, after a few drinks, he does nothing but talk about work and I just write everything down.

He tells me that to get into the bank's main vault you need two codes. The bank Manager always has one and a selected member of staff has the other. They've already told him that he'll have the other code for his last week as a going away present. Apparently it's a big deal if you get, "the code" in the banking world.

I wake up in the villa to my phone going at half six in the morning. This better be fucking important.

"Hello, who the fuck is this at this time, fur fuck sake?"

"It's Miss G Hugo."

"Oh sorry Miss G."

"No worries, I have some bad news for you Hugo. Davie Little was gunned down in Glasgow last night."

"Whit?"

"Unfortunately it's true. There's been a power struggle in Glasgow for a while now. I've spoken to my contacts up there and Glasgow is now in the hands of Tam Ferris. I've spoken to him this morning and he's not interested in the West of Scotland, only Central Scotland.

He mentioned your name and would like to work with you Hugo. He's heard about what you've done down here and wants you to run that coast as well as you've ran this one. I told him that I'd be reluctant to let you leave, but it's up to you of course."

"Christ I don't know what to say here. Davie was always good to me. Taking over his patch doesn't sound right, but going home? Can I get back to you Miss G and let all this sink in?"

"Of course Hugo, of course."

Fuck sake man, what do I do here? If Siham was here I'd stay 100%. I have nothing here now really. I spend my day in the bar, I have this lovely villa but it's not Scotland. I miss my pals, I miss the bookies and I miss Scotland in general. If I can get into that vault and get a retirement fund, then Scotland it is.

I 'phone Bruno and get him to collect young Kris to bring him to Hugo's. This is fucking on! I need to find out more about this Bank Manager and get that other code. This is one almighty job and carries serious prison time if caught, but by the way young Kris has been blabbing the past few weeks, the cunts will never expect it.

I arrive at Hugo's and Kris is already there with Bruno. Apparently he hasn't been home and fell asleep in the bar. His drinking is getting out of control.

"Wake that wee cunt up, Bruno"!

"Whit, whit, whit, whit......" says a confused Kris.

"Right you, you're ripping the fucking hole son. I've let you away with murder because of who your uncle is. No fucking more! You'll pay for your beer from now on. Ok?"

"Aye Hugo, nae bother. Sorry, man."

"I've got some bad news for you son. Yer uncle Davie got murdered last night. Shot in Glesga."

"Whit?"

"Unfortunately, it's true."

The boy has just woke up with a cunt of a hangover to be told that his uncle has been murdered. Probably not the best of things to waken up to, but he's in for an even bigger shock in the next five minutes.

"Right, you're going back to Scotland next week, correct?"

"Aye Hugo, I am"

"Right, here's what's going to happen. I'm coming with you, but I'm taking whatever is in your bank's vault with me."

"Eh?" says a confused and barely half awake Kris.

"I need the name and address of the Bank Manager wee man. When you get your code next week, you're going to give me it and I'll sort the Bank Manager out."

"Eh, how do you know about the codes."

"I know everything Kris, you like to talk some amount of pish when you're drunk son. You'll fly back with me on a private jet and I'll get Tam Ferris to look after you as part of my deal for going home."

"Tam Ferris, bank vaults and private jets Hugo? Whit's goin' on here, fur fuck sake?"

That's it, I've made my mind up. Scotland here I come. I phone Miss G and thank her for everything. I tell her that I'll take Tam Ferris's offer of running the West Coast of Scotland drug trade - on the condition he looks after young Kris, because fucking Interpol will be looking for him after next week.

I need to sort one last meeting to tell everyone my plans. I let Mustapha, Pepe, Bruno and Kris know the time and location of the meet. I'll miss this place I really will. I'll miss looking at that Rock every day, but it's time to go home. I'll be leaving this place knowing that I've completely turned it around. It's thriving once again.

A couple of days go by and after a few phone calls with Tam Ferris, my escape plan to Scotland is in place. I just need to sort this end out. Kris informs me of the Bank Manager's name and address. Jonny Olivera-Kenyon of 25 Shrine Walk in Gibraltar. I've had him monitored round the clock to get to know his routine.

Kris gets his code for the vault in the morning, for the start of his last week. We just need that Bank Manager's one now and we're sorted. Everybody arrives at Hugo's for the meeting. Jesus puts on a lovely spread of Tapas for the table. There's wine, water, coffee and beers already laid out. Our last supper.

"Ok, guys, I have some news for everybody. I'm leaving Spain for good next week."

"What boss, no way?" says Bruno

"Yes, I've been offered my home patch back in Scotland Bruno, and it's too difficult to turn that down. I've done all I can do here and I've done what I set out to do and turned this place around.

I'm not leaving without giving you all a present though. One million pounds each!!" We're going to rob the main vault in Gibraltar's biggest bank this Friday, with the help of young Kris here."

"Are you sure about this Hugo, this little bastard is a pisshead," says Pepe

"Pepe, yes I'm sure. We need two codes to open the vault, Kris gets his tomorrow and I already have the Bank Manager under surveillance in Gibraltar as we speak. He has the other.

Mustapha, I need safe passage to Morocco with my money, on a rib, where myself and Kris will go straight onto a Private jet already arranged by Miss G. I have everything sorted already for our arrival in Scotland. I will bring your million with me on that rib, Mustapha.

Bruno and Pepe. I'll need a seperate rib to pick up three million pounds from the pier behind the bank. One for Bruno, one for Pepe and one for Jesus. I'm taking four million pounds back with me to Scotland, so that's eight in total we'll be taking.

I'll also need a ten strong gang Bruno, with two white Transit vans. They can take one million pounds also from the vault and divide that amongst the ten of them."

"Hugo, this is crazy!" says Pepe. How are you going to walk out of a bank in Gibraltar with Eight Million Pounds, well, Nine Million pounds and not get caught?"

"Pretty simple really, the Bank Manager, our gang and young Kris here are going to carry it out for me."

I tell everybody the full plan and they start to come round to my way of thinking. We're about to steal Nine Million Pounds from the biggest bank in Gibraltar. That's nothing to them and it'll be insured anyway, so the bastard's won't lose a penny in the end up. Kris is a nervous wreck but he'll come round.

Bruno wants to buy a fancy bar in Gibraltar with his money. Pepe is going to buy a huge bit of land and build a Villa with his and Mustapha is gonna invest his in the Hashish trade in Morocco and try to quadruple his money.

Miss G has been excellent about everything. She said that I can keep the villa but I told her that it would be too dodgy for me to come back here after this. I've asked her to give the bar to Jesus as well. He'll look after it properly.

Miss G has one last request from me and that is that she wants her own personal Limo to be able to drop me off at the Gibraltar border on Thursday night before the heist takes place. I couldn't say no to that. I'll be leaving Spain forever in style.

CHAPTER NINETEEN

THE GIBRALTAR BANK JOB

The next few days are spent saying my goodbyes to everybody. I arrange one last cheerio with Pepe, Bruno and Jesus at Hugo's. Kris is about to finish his supposed second last shift at the bank soon because he won't be attending his last one tomorrow. It's 4pm on Thursday and by this time tomorrow, all going according to plan, we'll be in Scotland.

It's a sombre affair in Hugo's. None of the guys want me to go, but needs must. We have a laugh about some of the stuff we've gotten up to together and I give them all my final hugs.

"Pepe, thank you for everything pal. You've been a great help to me since I've been here. I appreciate it all and please come and visit me in Scotland or jail haha. Depending how tonight goes."

"I will Hugo, I will," says a teary eyed Pepe.

"Jesus, this bar is now yours mate, enjoy it and embrace it. Thanks for everything as well."

"No problem Hugo, it was my pleasure."

"And - finally Bruno. I can't wait to hear about this bar in Gibraltar. You go over there and take over that place with your share of the money pal. I didn't have to do much with you running this coast for me. Thank you for everything as well."

"Don't mention it Hugo, you will always be my boss."

We look outside as a horn goes off and a stretch Limo is waiting outside the bar. I turn round and give the guys one last thumbs up and climb inside the Limo as the driver opens the door for me. As I get inside, there's a blonde woman with bobbed hair, black glasses on, long legs and wearing a white dress sitting opposite me.

"Hi Hugo, I'm Miss G."

"Haha, no way?"

"Yes, way!" I wanted to ride this last mile and a half with you to the border and meet the legend himself."

"Och, I'm no legend Miss G."

"You are to me Hugo. You've tidied this coast up, profits are through the roof and even the Guardia Civil won't come near us now on this coast because of you. You've been a breath of fresh air on this coast and I'm devastated that you're leaving us, but completely understand. Your Private Jet is ready in Morocco to take you home."

"Thanks for everything Miss G. You've been a great help to me as well and I won't forget that. I hope I can call on you for advice from Scotland, if I need it?"

"Call me for anything Hugo and I mean that."

We pull up to the border and Miss G gives me a massive hug and wishes me good luck. This is it, I can't come back to Spanish soil after tonight. I walk across the border into Gibraltar and head towards Casemates Square. I'm meeting Kris in a Bar called Allswells at 8pm. The first bit of the plan is about to come into fruition.

Kris is already there with his uniform on from the Bank. I get him a pint and explain what's about to happen.

"Och, no fucking way Hugo"!

"Yes way, just go with it ya wee dick. You're lucky I'm taking you anywhere with me the way you've been behaving recently. Just go with it and we'll be in Scotland tomorrow and everything will be fine ok?"

"Aye, right, ok."

Kris finishes his pint and we head to Rooke Car Park where there's two vans waiting with 5 members of the La Linea gang in each of them. We get Kris in the back of one of them, blindfold him, cable tie his hands and duct tape his mouth shut.

I go into the other van and two of the gang are dressed as Royal Gibraltar Policemen for the next phase. We then head off in convoy to Europa Point and more specifically, 25 Shrine Walk. Jonny Olivera-Kenyon's residence.

It's finally starting to get dark but we hold off at Europa Point until it's completely dark and then slowly drive round the corner to his residence. We park at the little Mosque just out of sight and the two gang members dressed as Policeman leave the van and head towards his house.

(Knock knock knock knock)

"Hello Officers, what can I do for you?"

"Mr Jonny Olivera-Kenyon?"

"Yes, that's me?"

"There's an issue with the vault at the bank. We've been instructed by our boss to come and collect you. Our colleagues are currently in contact with the Guardia Civil in La Linea and they are trying to contact a Kris Little so that we can all meet at the bank to sort this out. "

"Ah yes, that'll be correct. Kris has the other codes for this week. Let me just grab the envelope with the codes, and a jacket. I'll be with you in two minutes."

The Bank Manager comes out of his house and the gang members explain that their Police Car is round the corner. As they walk round the corner, they grab him, put him to the floor, duct tape his mouth, cable tie his hands and put a blindfold on him. They then throw him in the back of the same van as Kris.

The two vans then head off back to Europa Point. The reason I chose Europa Point is because it's the most Southerly point in mainland Europe and there's nothing there. As it's pitch black, you can see ca's coming from hundreds of metres away. I needed to let our bank manager friend know what was about to happen.

I open the back door and get him and Kris out; take off their blindfolds and cut the duct tape off their mouths. We all have balaclavas on, so he can't see our faces. I let him know in only the best way I know how, just how this whole thing is about to go down. Straight to the fucking point!

"Mr Olivera-Kenyon and Mr Little, I know you probably both have no clue what is going on here, so I'm about to tell you. Tonight, I'm going to take Nine Million pounds from your vault. Here's what's going to happen.

At the stroke of midnight, we'll leave this location. Yourself and Kris will open the bank as normal and we'll all go inside and close the doors behind us. If you trigger any alarms, I will fucking shoot you both, do you understand?"

"Yes, yes" says Jonny. He's shaking like a leaf.

"Yes, no alarms," says Kris

"You will put your codes in to open the vault Jonny and then Kris will put his in. Once it's open, both of you will help these men to put Eight Million pounds in 32 Blue bags containing £250,000 in each bag.

Once that is done, you will then make another 4 seperate Red bags up with £250,000 in each, for my colleagues here to share amongst themselves. We will then all load up the two ribs at the back of the pier. The one on the right, with 20 Blue bags, containing Five Million pounds. The one on the left, with 12 Blue bags, containing Three million pounds plus 4 Red ones containing a Million.

You will both then secure the vault, the alarms and close the bank up - then, we'll all just walk out the bank like nothing's happened.

Jonny, you will get in the rib on the left and Kris will get in the one on the right. Providing everything goes as planned, nobody will die tonight or be harmed in any way shape or form. Does everybody understand?"

"Yes, yes we understand" say Kris and Jonny.

I send one of the vans down to the local chinese to get everybody food and we sit about eating until it the clock hits midnight. We then drive down Europa Road, down past the Casino and the famous "Rock Hotel" where John Lennon and Yoko Ono stayed when they got married here. We then head along Queensway to the Bank.

Once outside the Bank we sit for ten minutes with all the lights off to make sure there's no movement. We then pull all our balaclavas over our faces again and I instruct a gang member to take off both their blindfolds and cut the cable ties off their wrists. I keep their mouths gagged for now, until we get inside in case the Bank Manager screams.

We all make our way into the Bank without a hitch and no alarms go off. The Bank Manager then opens all the gates leading to the Vault and him and Kris then put their codes in. Jonny then opens the Vault and what a site to behold it is. There's fucking millions in there!! The team all start stuffing the Red and Blue bags with the £10,000 bundles of notes.

Once all the bags are packed with the money they all get cable ties off and dropped behind the front door. It's about a fifty metre walk to the pier, where the Ribs are waiting with the drivers. I get all the gang, plus Jonny and Kris to help with the bags. We load up the one on the left first and then the one on the right.

Jonny and Kris then secure the vault, the gates and the bank. The two drivers head back to La Linea with the empty vans to meet the rib with the Four Million pounds on it and the remaining gang members, along with Jonny, get on the rib on the left.

They'll head back to La Linea, meet Bruno with three million pounds and keep a million to split between the ten gang members. Jonny will then go with the gang to a safe house and he'll get dropped off at the Gibraltar border at 9am. By that time, we'll be in Scotland safe and sound when he raises the alarm.

The guys on the rib bound for La Linea get on board theirs. Jonny is blindfolded and his hands cable tied again. The rest of us all take our balaclavas off. Kris gets on my rib with me and our driver. I give the guys from La Linea one final wave and they set off back to Spain. Me, Kris, our driver and Five Million Pounds all head in the direction of Morocco.

I take one last look at the beautiful and majestic Rock behind me. I know I'll never see it again in the flesh and wipe a tear from my eye. I'll be in Bonnie Scotland in around four hour's time though. I just can't wait to get home.

CHAPTER TWENTY

THE JOURNEY HOME

We pull in to Morocco with no hiccups and Mustapha is there to greet myself and Kris. I throw him 4 Blue bags and tell him that his Million pounds is in them, to which he smiles. He places them in the back of a Mercedes car and instructs the driver to meet us at the landing strip. We bundle the other 16 into the back of a van and Mustapha drives us and the money to our awaiting Private Jet.

We arrive at the landing strip and put the 16 bags inside the plane. I tell Kris to go and wait on the plane so I can talk to Mustapha.

"Mustapha, thank you for everything Sir. That Million pounds is a token of my appreciation. Pepe, Bruno and Jesus were afforded the same gesture for their loyalty and you are no different It's been excellent working with you my friend."

"You've been amazing for everybody Hugo, you really have. Safe journey."

"Yes, goodbye Mustapha."

"Bye, Hugo."

I get on the plane and the air stewardess for our flight closes the door. The engines roar and we're off. Scotland here we come.

"Fucking hell, Hugo, that was amazing man," says Kris

"Aye, it was that son, now let's get us hame."

"I honestly thought you were going to shoot me and fling me into the Straits of Gibraltar haha."

"There's fucking time yet son."

Kris gives me a sheepish look and shuts his mouth for the remainder of the flight. We arrive in Scotland in approximately three and a half hours. Tam Ferris has secured us to land at Turnberry

Hotel in Ayrshire. Apparently it used to be an RAF station there and they have a landing strip so we'll go in undetected to the local Polis.

Tam kidnapped the Manager of the Hotel and made sure the lighthouse area was out of bounds to all guests until we landed and got away. Tam has set up a safe house in Glasgow for young Kris to lay low for a wee while. A smile is strewn across my face at the prospect of being in my own bed in four hours time.

We arrive at Turnberry Hotel on time and as planned. As we come to a halt, four vehicles approach the plane. The stewardess opens the doors and we walk down the steps. This silver haired guy in a big trench coat walks towards me with his hand held out.

"You must be Hugo."

"That's right aye, you?"

"Ferris, Tam Ferris. Everything you asked for this end is in place Hugo, as planned."

"Good, thanks Tam."

"Not a problem. You must be Kris then?" Tam looks behind me at wee Kris

"Aye, Kris."

"Good, your car awaits son. Get into that Red BMW there and we'll look after you wee man."

Young Kris then turns to Hugo.

"I'll be awright Hugo, sure I will?"

"Aye son, you'll be fine, Tam here has gave me his word."

"Thanks for no' killing me, Hugo."

"Haha, right beat it you ya wee dick."

Kris gets into the BMW with a few of Tam's heavies and sets off for Glasgow.

"So. Hugo, you ready?" says Tam

"A wull be when they 16 Blue bags on that plane are loaded into the boot of that car, aye."

Tam gives his remaining heavies the nod to get the bags from the plane and load them into the boot of the car. I get into the front seat and Tam gets in the driver's one. The remaining two cars box us in and we set off in a three car convoy to my place.

"You've built yourself a bit of a reputation Hugo. You make big decisions and stick to your guns, I like that. I think me and you will work very well together here. It's only first thing on a Friday morning just now, so don't want to bug you about work just yet. Take the weekend off and I'll come and see you on Monday with our plan going forward."

"I know Davie getting murdered must've came as a bit of a shock to you Hugo. The truth is, he was a police informant. Why do you think he never did any jail time?"

"To think about it Tam, I did always wonder that, aye."

"It's not got out yet that he's deid, it's only you, me and Miss G that know about it along with the two boys I got to do him in."

"I told young Kris so a did Tam, he was his nephew, so he knows anaw."

"Why do you think he went away to Gibraltar to work Hugo? He was an informant as well and he's currently on his way to the same shallow grave his uncle is in."

"Aw, fur fuck sake Tam. No way man?"

"Aye way, the wee cunt canny keep his mooth shut when he's got a drink in him and was boasting to aff duty Polismen in Glesga about his hero Uncle's exploits. Davie shipped him off to Gibraltar to try and give up the booze and hideaway for a wee while. They were due to have a family reunion this weekend with the boy due back. They'll have that fucking reunion noo alright."

"I knew he talked pish with a drink in him Tam, but surely no?"

"Aye, they cost us Millions with their blabbing mooths to the Polis. They won't blab again, that's for sure."

Tam pulls up outside my house. His heavies unload the bags for me and I direct them to put them all into the spare room.

"Right Hugo, I'll see you Monday and we'll get started."

"Aye, sound, Tam."

Tam and his heavies all drive away in their three big motors, back up to Glesga. I kinda feel sorry for wee Kris, but if it's true and him and Davie were grasses then you live by the sword, you die by the sword. They made their beds and will need to lie in them now.

I've missed this wee place, the bookies, the pub and general all round feel of the place. I'll get a few hours kip and head doon the toon and see who's about. I think a few people will get a shock to see me back. I just hope I've made the right decision.

I get up around midday and flick the telly on. I've missed Jackie Bird on the telly. The flame haired goddess that she is, giving us the Scottish News. Look at her there in her satin blouse. I know she wants me staring through that telly.

After the Scottish News on the BBC is the National news, I'm not normally interested in all that shite and I'm about to turn it over when suddenly....

"Bank Robbery in Gibraltar!!" Masked Gang kidnap Bank Manager and young employee to steal record haul of Nine Million Pounds!!"

"No fucking way man!!" I shout

It's starts the report showing Jonny Olivera-Kenyon looking inside a half empty vault with Police everywhere. They then get Jonny on camera.

"What happened here Mr Olivera-Kenyon?" asks the reporter

"Well, I was kidnapped from my home last night, by two men claiming to be Police Office's."

He then continues to tell the reporter the whole fucking story and then the reporter sends it back to the presenter in the studio in London.

"With me now is Chief Superintendent Price from Scotland Yard. Chief Superintendent, what can you tell us?"

"Well, what we can tell you is that the young employee, Kris Little, is still missing or on the run. Kris is the nephew of a notorious Glasgow crime boss, Davie Little and both men's whereabouts are unknown at this moment, but we would be very keen to speak to both."

"Are you looking for anyone else at the moment?"

"We believe the other men involved were local because of their accents, but it was definitely a Scottish man that assisted them and we believe that to be Davie with the inside knowledge of his nephew. We know that Davie has connections down there and the mythical up until now, crime boss "Miss G" is believed to be it."

"Oh ya fucking dancer ye!!"

I'm cutting aboot the hoose with fucking ants in my pants. Have I just pulled off a fucking masterstroke here? I need to go for a walk doon the shore and then doon the toon to clear my heid. Nobody knows I'm hame so the toon is in for one almighty surprise.

CHAPTER TWENTY ONE

HOME SWEET HOME

My hoose is right next to the shore front and I can walk two miles in either direction and take in the cool sea breeze that hits the West Coast of Scotland. I actually walked out my front door and looked right and expected to see the Rock of Gibraltar but instead saw the Hills of Arran. Not a bad substitute to be fair.

I go left for a mile and then turn left again and head towards the town centre. The bookies and the pub are about 200 metres away now and the town is bustling. There's no way I'm going to get through the crowd without getting recognised but deep down, that's what I want. I've got about £3000 on me and decide to head towards the bookies, I fancy a bet.

I walk in and it's like I haven't even left the place. The usual suspects are in, Alberto, Donald, his brother and a few of the cooncil boys, John, Colin and Tony. As soon as they see me, they all mob me. There's one other fella in the corner with a Bunnet oan.

"Fuck sake Hugo, man, I cannae believe it," says Colin

"Aye, it's me boys, I'm back."

They all shake my hand and pat me on the back and genuinely look delighted to see me, well except Donald.

"Whit's up wae your chops, Donald?"

"You know whit's up wi' ma chops Hugo."

"Aw, dae a noo?"

"Helima got rid of me because of you."

"The fuck you going on aboot man?"

"Well, no' cause of you, Siham."

"You better choose your next words fucking carefully Donald or I'll punch yer cunt in right in front of everybody."

"Woah, woah, woah, Hugo, calm doon man,! says John.

Tony, John and Colin stand between them.

"When she died, part of Helima died too. I wanted her and her kids to come back here with me, but she wouldn't leave Siham she said. It's not just you that's lost the love of your life Hugo, I have too. She told me to live my life in Scotland now and forget about her, how can I?"

"Donald, fuck sake man, how is any of this my fault?"

"You were the big shot over there and I didn't want that life. If only we'd have come home, or you'd picked somebody else to go down there with you then I wouldn't be in this state."

"Awright Donald, you're right. I should've sent you home earlier, I'm sorry about that."

"Och it's done noo, we both have to live with broken hearts."

Everybody moves out the way and the bookies goes back to normal. I walk up to the counter expecting auld Roberto, but completely forgot that not only did he retire, but he died no' that long ago and instead I'm confronted with this wee smug looking specky guy and I canny mind the wee cunt's name.

"Awright son, whit was your name again, wee man?"

"It's Thomas."

"Oh aye, Tam. Right Tam, £500 on trap 2 at Shawfield, to win."

I'm gonna have some fun with this boy. I manage to rinse the first £3000 of that Gibraltar money. I've only got another £4 million to try and launder through here now haha. This Tam is some boy, it's like it's his own money he's having to pay out. He'll no' last long in here with that attitude, or maybe he will. He'll be cannon fodder for oor patter in here.

After a few hours gambling the boys all head over to the pub and ask if I'm coming. I say aye, but let them know that I don't drink anymore. It seems Donald has beat me to the punch and told the boys the story.

We get over to the pub and there's a young lassie serving the pints. Again it's strange no' seeing auld Sadie behind the bar, but there's a photo of her next to the till the poor auld bugger. I introduce myself to the new barmaid.

"Hello there, hen"!

"Oh hello stranger, what's your name?"

"His name's Hugo," says Alberto from the end of the bar

"I can talk for myself thank you Alberto."

The wee Italian is staring away at the barmaid, he's clearly holding a torch for her.

"Hugo eh? I've heard folk in here talking about you. I'm Mel."

"Well, hiya Mel, can I put £500 behind the bar please and buy everybody their drink for night as a welcome home gift?"

"Of course you can Hugo, of course you can. A welcome home gift? Aye, I thought you stayed in Spain?"

"That's right, I did."

The pub is bouncing as word gets round the toon that it's a free bar. I'm sitting with the boys when a familiar face appears to thank me for the drink.

"Hugo!! Great to have you back in the town."

"Terry, how are you doing, darling?"

"Aye, I'm fine Hugo, I'm sat oor there wi' Janice fae the Charity shop and Tina fae the bookies if you want to join us?"

"Och, I better no; leave the boys Terry, they give me it stinking."

"Cheers anyway darling. How's wee JJ getting on?"

"Aye, he's at the school now. He's always looking out for you still walking through the toon haha."

"Well I probably owe him a wee bit of money noo, here, give him that £20 fae his uncle Hugo."

"Och, yer some man Hugo, so you are."

Donald's still continuing to give me the cold shoulder really, so I leave him to it. I'm not going to fall out with him, but if he blames me for Helima leaving him, then so be it. At least he's no' taking it out on her. He should just do I what I did and count his blessings that she was in his life at all for even that short space of time.

I see that guy with the bunnet on again - that was in the bookies earlier - sat at the table next to Terry, so I go over and introduce myself.

"Hello, Sir."

"Hello, young man."

"We haven't me. I'm Hugo."

"Hello Hugo, I'm James."

"Ah, you're Irish?"

"Dat's right, from a wee place West of Cork called Ballincollig."

"What brings you here James?"

"I visits me friend a few times a year. the local Priest here, Father Jackson."

"Ah I see, I saw you in the bookies earlier, do you like a wee flutter Sir?"

"I don't mind a wee gamble here and there my boy."

"Well, we might just be pals then my friend. It's a free bar tonight sir, on me, you get fired into that Irish Whiskey they have up there on that top shelf."

"Irish Whiskey? When in Scotland my boy, you have the proper Whisky sure?"

I leave the Irishman and head back to the table with the boys. Colin has since departed as Sanny has came in and dragged him to the other end of the pub away from the boys. Alberto is sitting at the end of the bar watching Mel's every move and it's good to see Terry out and managing to get a babysitter for wee JJ.

The lassies from the textiles factory are all in as well and are up singing and dancing. Donna, Lisa, Kirsty, Jan, Babs, Debbie, Leanne & Lynsey.

It's great to be home it really is. This is where I belong. Home sweet home. I leave the pub a happy man and take a long walk along the shore front again back home. It's great to see everyone again as well. I flick the kettle on and decide to have a wee coffee whilst watching the news before bed.

"The headlines tonight in Scotland," says oor Jackie Bird. "Two bodies have been found tonight in a shallow grave on the outskirts of Glasgow, believed to be that of notorious crime boss Davie Little and his nephew Kris..."...

THE END

The story "Hugo" was by Scott Alcroft

I'd like to dedicate this book to my two children, Paige and Aiden.

I'd also like to give a special mention to "The Bunnet" book club who without your perserverance and help behind the scenes, this Book wouldn't have been possible. x

Printed in Great Britain
by Amazon

33125130R00050